UNTOLD STORIES

Beachy Head

© K. J. Varney

Sheila Ryan

S. B. Publications

First published in 2010 by S. B. Publications
Tel: 01323 893498
Email: sbpublications@tiscali.co.uk
www.sbpublications.co.uk

ISBN 978-185770-364-1

Designed and Typeset by EH Graphics (01273) 515527

Front cover photo: K. J. Varney
Back cover photo: K. J. Varney

Contents

View from the edge. © K. J. Varney

Chapter 1

Beachy Head

'I felt drawn over the edge at Beachy Head.
This beautiful place invites you to die'

Louis de Bernieres

Beachy Head has enraptured the mind and influenced poetry of man for centuries. From the pike of the South Downs headland, the view is seamless seascape that varies with every visit. The dramatic 535 ft sheer white cliffs are a dazzling stark contrast to an expanse of pure blue, where nature appears to have invisibly stitched together the sea to the horizon.

Overlooking the English Channel, at the far end of the Seven Sisters chalk cliffs on the south coast of England, is one of England's most popular natural beauty spots, designated an Area of Outstanding Natural Beauty since June 1965. Des Lynam recently presented the spectacular panorama as a contender on ITV's search for Britain's Favourite View and on 12th November 2009 it officially became the South Downs National Park.

On the clearest of days, looking east, the scenery spans 40 miles past Eastbourne's picturesque beaches, town, and pier as far as Dungeness, Kent. To the west, the view extends 70 miles towards Chichester, Sussex and, occasionally, on the clearest of days, the Isle of Wight can be seen in the far distance. On more inclement days, the cliffs are shrouded in low lying mists with gusting cross winds that have shaped the cedar trees into an awry tilt towards the sea.

For most of the million people that visit the four miles of cliffs each year, it is a place to walk, relax and enjoy the landscape. But there lies in this natural beauty a chilling history. In passing, it is a place of awe and inspiration, but if you linger a little, chat to the locals or simply stay long enough on the headland, you may encounter a very different Beachy Head. This stretch of the cliffs has another, more notorious, reputation. Despite its magnificence, here is a deadly and tragic place that lures more suicide attempts, yearly, than anywhere else in the world. Most are successful.

Legend has it that there have been deaths on these cliffs since the 7th century.

View of Eastbourne. © K. J. Varney

In 666AD St Wilfrid, Bishop of York (634-709) whilst on a mission, was shipwrecked by a fierce storm at Beachy Head. Saxon pirates, who were notorious, merciless wreckers, attacked the crew as they floundered on the edges of the shore. Wilfrid prayed for salvation, battling his prayers against a

Countryside centre. © K. J. Varney

Pagan priest who, with evil intention, was urging the plunderers on. Despite ferocious fighting Wilfrid's faith held out. The Pagan priest, roaring in the frenzy, was fatally wounded by a stray slingshot. As he lay dying on the shingle beach, the wind suddenly changed direction and the tide began to rise, lifting the ship away from the shoreline and back out to sea.

Tree with awry tilt. © K. J. Varney

St Wilfrid went back to the north of England to continue his monastic work until 680AD, enforcing Roman rule of Christianity against the Scottish monks and building many monasteries of the Benedictine Order until Theodore, Archbishop of Canterbury, decided that he would subdivide the great diocese over which Wilfrid ruled. Wilfrid was incensed by the interference and fled to Rome for an audience with Pope Agatho and his papal council. The Pope decreed that the Archbishop had overreached his authority and sent back word that the diocese should remain as one. But, Theodore, King of Northumbria, refused to honour the papal decree and ordered Wilfrid to be detained at Bamburgh prison and from there exiled from his kingdom. St Wilfrid decided to return to Sussex where the word of God had not yet reached. Apart from a few Irish peasants, the local people were still gripped by Paganism. On his arrival he was horrified to witness the simple farmers and villagers hurling themselves from the cliffs at Beachy Head, wretchedly holding hands in lines of 40 to 50 people before stepping over the edge, to escape famine and drought that was ravaging rural England.

For six years, St Wilfrid is said to have taught those remaining how to fish and find alternative food while converting the last known Pagan lands of England to Christianity.

Detailed documentary evidence of falls and suicides has been recorded at Eastbourne's parish register since 1600, chronicling unique, true stories of terror and despair. Yet there have also been many untold stories of accidents, treachery and murder at the great cliff.

At Beachy Head the sheer power of nature and panoramic view of slate-blue sea blurring with the pastel horizon is quite simply breathtaking. From the highest cliff in the land, nature taunts you to test your nerve. Shimmy as close to the edge as you dare. The wise and the sympathisers drop onto their bellies and finger-pull to the edge, squinting in fear at the crumbling terrain, anxious to experience the danger but also relieved to pull back again to safety. Underestimate the danger at your peril.

Just sitting watching people as they stroll along the headland can evoke a terrible dread that echoes in an uneasiness, fluttering deep in your own essence, urging you to walk over and chastise complete strangers. Every foolishness is witnessed, from groups of teenagers larking around on the grassy verge pretending to push each other off, to tourists teasing friends by standing too close to the edge.

Number 13 bus. © K. J. Varney

During the summer months, the numbers of visitors consistently rise at Beachy Head. From May onwards a tourist bus travels in both directions, from Eastbourne to the east and Birling Gap to the west, every twenty minutes. With each bus journey comes the opportunity for anyone to access these beautiful cliffs of despair. The ice-cream man in his glacial palace, parked next to the Samaritans' warning board, has often been a source of confession and is practised at spotting people at risk. Yet the bus drivers have no such responsibility. With the bustling summer season, they ferry the tourists, poets, artists, walkers, bird-watchers and the like to this place of stunning definition. Slipped among them are the lost sorrowful souls, intent on leaving this world.

The majority of suicides take place directly above the ornate, red and white lighthouse, almost as a sacrificial offering to it. It takes a terrifying seven seconds to reach the rocky shore below that, in most places, is unsurvivable.

Yet suicide, the final hushed taboo of society, wanders as lonely as the ghosts of the forgotten, haunting Beachy Head. A tragic demise so terrifying to contemplate it has been banished to the bleakest annals of language. An unspoken reality of such hopeless despair that, across the world, it still attracts prejudice, rarely discussed openly, for fear of creating a profound sense of unease. The scandal attached to taking one's own life; suicide, parasuicide, self-murder, self-sacrifice all shocking terms that are used, that may be simply denying the fantasy of, perhaps, a final wish fulfilled. It is considered such an odious act that is still judged in a court of law to determine a guilty or innocent plea on the departed as a candid day of reckoning for those left behind.

Until 1961, suicide was considered an unlawful act. Despite the abolition of this act, relatives and friends, known as 'survivors of suicide', still have to face the criminal process: a court of law, intent, victim, inquest, jury, and verdict. Death certificates are often recorded as open verdicts, misadventure or accident which blurs the true statistics of how many people perish, by choice, at the foot of the cliffs.

Rarely is a public suicide witnessed at Beachy Head, but it's impossible to spend any length of time without looking at others with just a tinge of suspicion. Wondering about their intentions as they stand close to the edge, staring out to the mellow stillness. Their bodies swaying in the wind, teasing the onlooker. They are alone, no camera, unmoved by the tiny floral memorials that appear at the most deadly spots. The turf worn thin under their feet from the sheer numbers that have chosen that same spot to expel their last seven seconds of breath, tumbling to their deaths onto the shingle beach below. Locally, this one fatal precipice is known as the launch pad.

On a November afternoon in 2007 I'd arranged to meet with coastguard, Stuart McNab, Station Officer for the Eastbourne Cliff Rescue Team, on the cliff top. As we were chatting we spotted the chilling sight of a man who was standing on the launch pad. He had bobbed under the meagre barrier and stood, oddly motionless, on what appeared to be the very edge of the world. He was staring straight ahead, the breeze gently billowing his coat. The figure looked surreal, a dark silhouette against an unusually bright blue winter sky. Watching him closely his stillness had a statue quality, a visual artistic deterrent to any other would-be jumper, evoking images of a clothed Antony Gormley sculpture, staring wistfully over the ocean, hypnotised, the soul already departing. As we watched him for a while, it was difficult to assess his intention, even if he didn't mean to jump that day he was perilously close to the edge.

Stuart began a slow measured walk towards the man. Hoping not to startle him, he asked if he was okay, trying to convince him to come away from the edge. The man turned his head, briefly, in response: 'It's not what you think,' he replied, before looking back out towards the distant horizon. Stuart stood quietly just feet from him. Seconds later the man sat down on the grassy verge, still dangerously close to the sheer drop. Worried that he may decide to jump or even accidentally fall, Stuart calmly left him to call up the rest of his team.

But as he did so, the man stood up, staring wildly after him, and stepped away from the edge, before storming off in what appeared to be frustration with the interference in his life's choice. He was later seen sitting in his car before finally leaving the area, thankfully in one piece, for that day anyway.

Beachy Head holds mysteries of nature and man. On spring days as the sun begins to warm the earth, the migrant birds fill the air with sweet dawn chorus. Chiffchaffs swirl with Willow Warblers and the sweep of chalk downland breaks into vibrant colour with exotic orchids. Delicate painted lady, Adonis blue, and striking clouded yellow butterflies dance on the cowslips and hedgerow.

As autumn settles, elderberries and blackberries wave their nectar at the visiting Wheatears and Thrushes, fattening for their journey to warmer climes. The seascape stretches its view for all to see, widening with the rise of each new day. Yet for all this splendour bursting to life those most hopeless cannot see beyond the dark shadows of their souls.

CHAPTER 2

The Light

It is thought that a light has shone in some form over the cliffs since 1670 often for very different reasons. Historical accounts include evidence that light was used to warn ships away from the shallow waters and jagged coastline. For more sinister reasons lights were often attached to cows in order to deliberately mislead passing ships, who would believe the light was a signal

Beachy Head and Belle Tout lighthouse. © K. J. Varney

Torch. © K. J. Varney

from another boat on the horizon. For the captains this would generally mean that the area close to the shore was safe. However, the closer they sailed to the shoreline, the sooner the boat would become grounded on the rocks, and usually lives would be lost. The booty spilled from the hulls would then be shared out amongst a grateful local community.

But with so many ships floundering a petition was sent to the Crown in 1691and referred on to The Corporation of Trinity House, in charge of all lighthouses in England and Wales, imploring their brethren to erect a lighthouse at Beachy Head, a plea that was ignored for more than 100 years. Trinity House's connection with seamarks dates to the Seamarks Act of 1566 which gave their brethren powers to set up 'So many beacons, marks and signs for the sea...whereby the dangers may be avoided and escaped and ships the better come into their ports without peril.' With limited funds Trinity House did however allow private enterprises to erect guiding lights along the coast.

Early in the 18th century, Parson Jonathan Darby, decided to construct a more permanent warning light after an 800-ton schooner was grounded with no survivors. Since 1692, he had been a curate serving his parish of St Michael's church in Litlington then, later, as Rector of Wilmington, and Parson of Friston and East Dean, just a few miles inland. It was his duty to bury the bodies of all the sailors that were washed up on the shores of East Sussex. The wrecked schooner finally drove him to find a way to protect the seafarers from further danger.

Using just a chisel, pick, and axe, he began working on an existing smugglers' cave. From it he carved a series of tunnels into the cliffs and a chalk staircase which led up to it from the beach. One of the caves had a balcony 20 ft above the highest point of the water which could be reached from a chimney dug into the Downs. He used this chimney to fix a light that was protected from the sea and the gusty winds, to direct unsuspecting mariners away from the perilous waters. Inside the cave were some more carved steps that led to a large space that could house up to 35 people with a lookout that was 50 ft above the shingle beach. He also enlarged intricate tunnels, which had previously been used to store contraband, into dry storage for his spare lanterns and fashioned a bedroom where he spent many days sleeping after long nights watching over the sea. When he died in 1726, aged 59, a headstone was erected on his grave that reads:

> *'Here lies the body of*
> *Parson Darby M.A. Oxon*
> *Who died on 26th October 1726*
> *He was the sailors' friend'*

Belle Tout circa 1904. Courtesy of R. Wassell

Rumours persist, however, that he may also have taken advantage when ships ran aground and used the cave to hide treasured salvage. Certainly, after his death, the labyrinth hole was used by wreckers and smugglers to store their bounty; most of the cave was still accessible 200 years later, but cliff falls would finally remove all traces of his work. While the parson's crude efforts to blaze lights on the headland may have saved many mariners, frequent shipwrecks still continued around the foot of the cliffs. This was the case until a local squire and MP 'Mad Jack' Fuller (1757-1834), better known for his opulent lifestyle and outgoing personality, raised the cash to erect a lighthouse. A site was chosen overlooking the sea from the headland where the undulating cliff is 200ft lower than the sheerest point.

In 1828 he commissioned a small wooden hut with a single light to be built as a temporary beacon while the Belle Tout lighthouse was being constructed. When the lighthouse was completed in 1832, it stood 100 ft from the cliff edge which rises to 325 ft at this point. But Belle Tout has a less than heroic past. Engineer, James Walker, along with local architect, William Hallett, designed the tower to stand at just 50 ft in height. They installed an Argand lamp which bounced a beam from reflectors on a revolving platform in a long flash every two minutes. When they had built the tower, they had failed to calculate that its short height would be affected by the low-lying clouds and seasonal mists which obscured the light, nor did they consider the proximity of the lighthouse to the crumbling cliff edge. Ships continued to flounder and, in 1893, 85,000 tons of chalk slid into the sea. An even heavier landslide in 1896 meant that Belle Tout was now just 70 ft from the cliff edge.

In 1899 Trinity House abandoned the ineffective tower and commissioned Sir Thomas Matthews to design a replacement at the foot of the cliffs. (endnote: Woodman R, Wilson J (2002) *The Lighthouses of Trinity House* Thomas Reed Publications GB)

Belle Tout passed into private hands in 1923, becoming a social hub where distinguished guests such as King George V and Queen Mary were treated to fantastic views from this unique residence. During the Second World War the glamour was gone and Belle Tout was alleged to have been requisitioned by Canadian troops to be used as target practice. Elizabeth Wright of Hampden Park, after years of speculation, finally found proof that this was not the case. Writing in the local *Argus* newspaper she reported that the damage had been caused accidentally.

She quotes from James Donne's Wayfarer's Diary, as published in the *Sussex County Magazine* in June 1947: 'I last saw Belle Tout empty, but undamaged, in the summer of 1941... ... A few months later everything had changed. Tanks were skirmishing all along the downs and about 200 yards east of Belle Tout a firing range was being constructed. It consisted of a light railway crossing the valley formed by two hills, on one of which stands the old lighthouse. The rails ran part of the way up the hill, finishing in a dug-out. Inside this was an old car-minus tyres-and the back wheel was used as a winch to tow a life-sized target of a tank along the rails. Soon afterwards firing began and by 1942 it was incessant from dawn to dusk, never stopping, even on Sundays. Almost every kind of gun was in use, from cannon to light howitzers, and training crews arrived in relays. In theory the lighthouse should have been untouched, being out of the field of fire; in practice we could see shells bursting around it,

Belle Tout war damage. *Courtesy of R. Wassell*

Belle Tout foundations on cliff edge. Courtesy of R. Wassell

Belle Tout lantern room now.
Courtesy of R. Wassell

and with a telescope, see the deep scars in the masonry from bursting shrapnel....Day after day I watched in agony of this famous structure, continually being hit by (live) shells fired wide of the mark. (Any shells that missed the tank target were supposed to fall harmlessly into the sea). The granite rocks withstood this fierce punishment all through 1942, but by 1943 great rents had appeared in the structure and one could see daylight through the building.' (endnote: The Argus 23/01/08:Belle Tout NOT used for practice. Pub 23/01/08)

The lighthouse fell into dereliction for seven years following this battering but was rescued in 1950 from demolition by Eastbourne council who officially named it as a Grade II listed building. In 1955 an architect, Edward Cullinan, fulfilled a vision to restore the lighthouse once more into a family home. After his death his widow Dorothea put the old lighthouse up for sale for £15,000.

The tower changed hands many times after that and was once occupied by a tenant in 1967 who, for unknown reasons, hanged himself from the spiral staircase. By 1985 the sale price had risen to £50,000. In 1986, the tower was the star of a TV drama featuring in Fay Weldon's cautionary tale, *The Life and Loves of a She-Devil.* The transformation and restoration of the lantern by the BBC for the three weeks filming pushed the value of the property to an unprecedented £350,000. Yet it remained unsold for two years until the Roberts family: Mark and Louise and their two children, Haven and Quinn, were tempted into restoring the interior with the aim of turning it into an exceptional bed and breakfast.

But on a drizzly November 4th night in 1998, a rumbling sound sent the family into a panic. The constant rain being lashed by a bitterly east wind was raging against the crumbling chalk cliff causing a landslide that sent great chunks of land to the sea below. Gathering the children under each arm Mark shouted to Louise to grab their pet dog as they ran barefoot for their jeep, driving across the Downs to safety. When they returned in the morning, white and grey dust was still rising over the headland. The lighthouse seemed to have survived the disaster, standing proud and undamaged, but it was teetering perilously just 9 ft from the cliff edge. Mark knew immediately that they now had little choice, either give up their dream, cut their losses and move away, or try to find an expert engineer that could lift the building and move it further away from the brink. It became a trade-off for the family. The cost to move it 55 ft way from the cliffs was a staggering £250,000. A South Downs Charitable Trust was set up to raise some of the funding, if they accepted this help, it meant giving the public access to their family home. They felt they had no choice.

The unique work to move the building inch by inch began in March 1999, with the aim of preserving it for at least another 50 years. The family continued to live there, though for some reason, the visitor centre was never opened and their dream of a bed and breakfast never came to fruition. When the Roberts family decided to give up their dream and sell the lighthouse in September 2007, there were outcries at the exaggerated price tag of £850,000 which put it beyond any reasonable offer by the Belle Tout Lighthouse Preservation Trust, a charitable trust set up by Rob Wassell to preserve the building. (http://www.belletout.org) Days before the trust could make a tender to save the building for the people of Eastbourne a bid was accepted, from a mystery buyer, for the full asking price. But in January 2008 that original offer fell through and the new asking price dropped to £595,000. It was finally sold to David and Barbara Shaw in April 2008.

The fate of this troubled building is an ongoing story, its guiding light over the seas was extinguished in 1899, yet 111 years later the lighthouse still holds a fascination with the public. The new owners have lovingly restored and refurbished the building ready for a spring 2010 opening of a stunning bed and breakfast, despite the fact that the ocean may eventually reclaim the lighthouse where it will, undoubtedly, perish on the rocks below.

Taking two years to construct, designer Sir Thomas Matthews' new lighthouse at the base of the cliffs finally began operating on 2nd February 1902. Since then, the red and white, candy-striped lighthouse at the foot of the headland has shone a constant nocturnal light of two white flashes every 20 seconds. The life-saving beam spans out 26 miles as a warning to seafarers, guiding them away from the treacherous seas and the sheer vertical white cliffs that stand 535 feet behind it.

To simply view or photograph the lighthouse from above entails a heart-stopping lean over the collapsing cliff edge which erodes, randomly, at an average of 18 to 36 inches a year. Its pillar box lantern is barely visible unless you take a thrilling, dangerous risk to capture a rare camera shot as it guards the sea.

For the sailors passing by, Beachy Head lighthouse by day looks like a tiny, discarded, floating, Victorian toy but as evening falls it appears alive and earnest in its search for stray ships. Yet Beachy Head, the last traditional rock tower built by Trinity House, stands magnificent at 153 ft. Just 16 feet smaller than Nelson's Column, it beams its life-saving light, 20 nautical miles out to sea.

Keeping a silent vigil the keepers remained devoted to the task of saving the lives of seafarers. Their isolation was rewarded whenever the 'thank you' horn sounded in the distance, from grateful passing ships, no longer tolled a penny per lighthouse by Trinity House for their safe passage. When the keepers were commissioned to the lighthouse, they knew little of the rare nature of the building but few would fail to be touched or disturbed by the tragic history of Beachy Head. When more ships were wrecked at the foot of the cliffs, engineers worked tirelessly to improve the location and efficiency of the candle lamps, helping them to send warning messages deeper and further out to the ocean. Yet the land held no such change. Year in, year out the saddened, the mournful, the unlucky and the pitiful would find their way to Beachy Head, the light unable to touch them, warn or deter.

In the dark of night, the lighthouse does not illuminate the cliffs and this darkness is bleak and lonely. Sinister mists descend, shrouding and blurring the cliff edge. Late at night the atmosphere somehow feels different, more isolated. The lighthouse turns its back on you to do its work.

Belle Tout restored. Courtesy of R. Wassell

CHAPTER 3

Keepers of the light

Up until June 1983 three lighthouse keepers had kept a 24-hour watch on the sea around Beachy Head. This was not always the case. Since 1801, The Corporation of Trinity House, in charge of all English and Welsh lighthouses, instructed that there should always be three lighthouse keepers on duty. The reason for this decision was based on a terrible incident that took place at a remote rock lighthouse, in the southwestern corner of Wales.

It was on Smalls lighthouse, where just two keepers were on duty: Tom Howells and Tom Griffiths, who were well known to dislike each other and

Smalls Lighthouse. © R. Wassell

Tony Marsh PK. © Peter Ekin-wood, Eastbourne 1972

argued ferociously. The nature of the job meant that keepers were sometimes confined to tiny living quarters for months on end. There was no outside contact or communications, especially on the rock towers, which were positioned, mostly, far out in the ocean miles away from any shore. With very little to do with their free time apart from reading, playing cards, or maybe go fishing on rare fine days, it was imperative that the keepers got on well. These two clearly didn't and events intervened in a tragic way.

Bill James, Dick Packer and John Dobinson playing cribbage. © Chris Ware, Keystone Press Agency 1950s

Usually the keepers would be relieved of duty after one month on the tower, returning

Cleaning the lantern. © Assoc. Lighthouse Keepers

to their families onshore but fierce winter storms had meant that no relief boats could reach them. For four long months they remained isolated and embittered, their rows often growing ugly although there was never any evidence to suggest that their arguments spilled over into physical violence. One night, in 1801, as gales lashed against the lighthouse, the two men, once again, began arguing. After this particularly furious row, Tom Griffiths, so enraged, suddenly collapsed; as he fell to the floor he gashed his head on a metal lantern and died on the spot where he landed. Tom Howells could do nothing to save the man's life and immediately realised that, as there were no other witnesses around, he may easily be accused of murder. He had to do something drastic and decided that to protect his innocence he would have to keep the body at the lighthouse rather than committing the remains to a traditional eternal resting place at sea. Fearfully he looked around the lighthouse for anything he could use to conserve the body. Ripping out the interior kitchen cupboards he set about making a box; he put Tom's body into it, hauled the dead weight up the spiral stairway and with dreadful biting winds hampering him he finally lashed it to the railings on the external balcony of the lantern. He hoped the harsh cold weather would preserve the body and lessen the stench from the decaying corpse. Next to it, he flew a distress flag and made sure the light shone brightly each night onto the troubled seas.

John Dobinson AK circa 1950s.
© Chris Ware, Keystone Press Agency 1950s

In the distance, passing ships noted the 'strange object' in their Captains' Logs but never raised the alarm. Trinity House frantically kept trying to send relief boats out but they were beaten back each time by the unrelenting storms which, by now, had swept crashing waves over the gallery, smashing the crude coffin to

Lighting the tonite charges. © Chris Ware, Keystone Press Agency 1950s

fragments. Tom Griffiths' shrouded, mouldering body was now hanging across the balcony, one arm grotesquely caught in the railings.

When a rescue crew finally did arrive, the squall had subsided and in the distance they could just make out the wretched sight of the body. Full of fear and dread they thought the ravaged corpse was waving them onto the perilous rocks. By the time they reached Tom Howells, loneliness and terror had made him unrecognizable; they found a broken man who had slowly but surely gone mad. As a result of that pitiful event up until the automation of all lighthouses in 1998, there were always three keepers to every lighthouse for every shift.

Relief day - Dick Packer handing down John Dobinson's things. © Chris Ware, Keystone Press Agency 1950s

At Belle Tout Barbara Scott has vivid accounts taken from her grandmother Emily Barnby diaries. Emily's father Chessman Barnby, a jolly and popular man with a big bushy beard, and her mother Agnes moved to Belle Tout when he was made Chief lighthouse keeper on 20th January 1874. Emily was just two years old and Agnes was heavily pregnant with her ninth child. Life must have been harsh high on the clifftop but Emily's tale is full of carefree happiness. She recalls:

'We kept chickens and a pig, and bought milk from a local farm. Father grew vegetables in the garden. Once he decided to collect some gulls' eggs so he went to where the cliff was a little lower and lay on his stomach and, with a long rod with a net on its end, got up the eggs.' The family were mostly self-sufficient, Agnes making her own yeast and ketchup, storing them twelve bottles at a time. The children all helped when it came time to kill the pig.

John Dobinson loading tonite charges.
© Fox Photos Ltd. London 1948

'The pig was killed in the garden and hung in the shed before being treated. It was put in a tub of hot water and scraped until it was white, then hung up to a hook in the ceiling. Father would cut it and take out the inside - oh, it was a nasty smelly business! There was fat to render down for lard, yards of sausages to prepare and make, spare ribs to bake, the stomach to clean and fill with pudding mixture and boil. When ready, Father would cut the hams and shoulders and cure them and they would hang on hooks in the kitchen.' That wasn't all that was stored in the garden shed. Emily remembers once 'the wreck of a vessel broke up nearby. It apparently had a mixed cargo, as oranges, barrel bungs, corks and nutmegs were strewn along the shore, which I believe lasted mother a long time: also planks from which father had enough to make good his garden fences.' By now it was 1878 and Agnes had given birth to her tenth child George. The eldest two brothers, John and William, had already left home. The smaller children spent their days playing on the cliff top as their father could no longer afford the 6d a week each for them to attend school. Emily's happiest memories were when John came home to visit them at Christmas. He would make the long journey from London by train then walk the five miles from Eastbourne often in the dark.

Bill James on washing-up duty.
© Assoc. Lighthouse Keepers 2007

'If a gale was blowing the last 100 yards of steep incline were accomplished by scrambling on hands and feet. The rays from the lantern would make a good target to aim for when he reached the top of Eastbourne hill.'

One year he arrived with sugar toys to hang on the Christmas tree and took his little brothers and sisters out to gather evergreen, spindlewood and mistletoe to make festive decorations. Later she recalls him helping them hang their stockings which were later filled with nuts and oranges. The tiny rooms of the lighthouse must have been filled with the happy laughter of all those children. By April 1888 Emily's father, aged just 58, had become so ill from heat stroke seeing to the powerful lighthouse lantern that he and Agnes retired to Ramsgate leaving Belle Tout for the last time.

For the lighthouse keepers who had manned Beachy Head their families were housed on the land for which they were probably grateful. The discovery of bodies at the foot of the rock-face posed a heartbreaking dilemma. Whilst they guarded the ocean and seafarers, they were helpless witnesses to the futile desperation that was happening on the cliff face. On five occasions three bodies were recovered in a single day, including February 27th 2010.

Although their purpose was to keep vigil on the sea, the structure of the lighthouse, which is divided into seven floors all connected by a spiral staircase, has views from the living quarters and bedrooms through small square windows directly onto the cliffs. Sitting 550 ft out to sea, the most the keepers

Lighthouse. © K. J. Varney

could do was to alert the police and coastguard, and then silently observe as dramatic cliff rescues or recoveries were made. Because of the unique terrain and shrouded mists around Beachy Head, these rescues took anywhere from half an hour to four days and were often perilous. The keepers could only watch and wait as the rescuers, at fearsome risk to their own lives, defied the elements and nature in their grim task.

Life was a harsh existence for the keepers, isolated from their families on rock towers for weeks on end, often stranded by lashing weather long after they should have started their shore leave. Ted Frostick remembers well the short time he served on Beachy Head:

'I'd served on six stations, and I liked Beachy Head least of all. The tower was the last lighthouse to be electrified by Trinity House, so as there was no power we had to hand pump our oil and water.'

The romantic, almost magical, notion of the keepers simply maintaining the light as they stared out over the ocean for hours on end is far from the truth:

'It was necessary to wind the mechanism every hour, to keep the lens rotating, and also to pump up the oil pressure occasionally. We always had an incandescent mantle ready, in case of a flare up. Sometimes carbon would build up in the burner. And then, instead of the oil vapour going through the mantle, it would flare out at the side; and usually damage the mantle. In my experience, this occurred most nights; sometimes several times. And when it happened the light would fail. If we were lucky we could just change the mantle. But sometimes we had a blockage, and it was necessary to change the entire lamp. As you imagine, time was of the essence.'

Apart from keeping the light going throughout the night, Beachy Head also has frequent low mists and fog, which diminish the visibility for passing ships:

'During fog we detonated Tonite charges to warn shipping. They were 4oz sticks of explosive, similar to dynamite. They were detonated every 5 minutes. We didn't get much sleep those nights.' Heating in the whole lighthouse was supplied by two small gas rings that were also used for cooking.

In the middle of February 1970, as a young man then of just 22 years, David 'Dai' Woosnam still has one enduring memory from his brief time as an assistant lighthouse keeper at Beachy Head. He had been posted there after a short time at St Catherine's Point on the Isle of Wight.

'I had my rail warrant from my home in Porth in the Rhondda Valley and was sent the address of a family in Eastbourne where I was to lodge for one night. They would explain to me about the tides and where I was to walk from the next day. The next morning after breakfast, carrying my provisions from the

Ligththouse keepers' view to the cliffs.
© H.M. Coastguard

local ships chandler, I set off along the rocks all the way to the lighthouse.'

The tide was out and Dai was greeted at the foot of the stone steps by the Principal Keeper and his assistant Gordon Hartnell. Both men were experienced keepers in their late forties. Dai was tasked with every menial job that was needed from making tea to walking the rock-strewn shore into town for post and provisions.

'I recall that first night it was deeply impressive; the towering cliffs seemingly about to fall and submerge you, and the beam going around every few seconds with an intensity and power that meant you could have performed intricate brain surgery on someone badly injured and trapped on the ledge.'

But the light didn't help him one grave night.

'I will never forget it. Gordon was in his quarters resting when we heard his quiet painful cries for help. We found him gripping his chest from a heart attack.'

Dai ran to the phone calling the coastguard, the tide was moving surely towards the beach and only a lifeboat could reach them.

'In came the RNLI lifeboat up to the landing. It was pitch dark, save for our demented beam lighting up events, it seemed, every few seconds. The biggest problem was getting Gordon down to the boat. He was about 16 stone and there was no way he could be brought down the incredibly tight spiral staircase. So the coxswain decided to bring him out through the window on a sort of breeches buoy. Gordon was put into what looked like a straightjacket.' (Probably a Neil Robertson stretcher, an emergency extrication stretcher made of canvas with wood backing pieces which form a splint around the patient and guide ropes at the foot and head.)

Stretcher going down. © H.M. Coastguard

'The guys pushed him upright and wedged his whole body out through the

1984 International Year of Peace. © K. J. Varney

reinforces the shame that has been attached to the subject of suicide since the Middle Ages.

However, despite the Samaritans sign at Beachy Head encouraging the sad and lonely to call for help from the local phonebox, it was clear that something else was needed on the cliffs.

The Beachy Head Chaplaincy Team (BHCT) began their vigil on the 8th August 2004 after founder, Parson Ross Hardy, had 'a vision by God one morning in July 2003.' Out of this inspiration came a mission to set up a dedicated prevention strategy that would position the team as a new redeeming light on the cliff top. A group was quickly established as a visible presence on the headland, offering help and advice to anyone in need. Their patrols, at first, were operated with 14 frontline volunteers, all active members of local churches in the parish, and dedicated to the 'statement of faith' as set out by the Christian charity, Christ Church of Healing and Counsel. Supported by seven aftercare volunteers and an intercessory prayer team of 42, the shifts were shared by the members, who covered the hours from 6.45pm to midnight, seven days a week. There were also regular daytime patrols on Fridays and Saturdays.

War Memorial. © K. J. Varney

In addition, there was a 24-hour on-call team that responded to calls from Sussex Police, staff at the Beachy Head Pub, Birling Gap Hotel, and members of the public.

On the tiny stretch of coastline that has seen more deaths than it deserves, token inanimate objects

Crosses mark the place two people jumped from. © K. J. Varney

Peace plaque. © K. J. Varney

have been placed to curb the path to self-destruction. Plinths and biblical messages strew the way. A peace path built in 1987 leads directly to the cliff edge, even the disabled can now get access. At the beginning of the peace path is a United Nations plaque nailed onto a memorial stone laid to signify the purchase, by the council, of the Downland in 1929. Beside it are two park benches with brass plates inscribed: Year of Peace

A memory card attached to the meagre fence. © K. J. Varney

Prayer for peace. © K. J. Varney

Chaplains. © K. J. Varney

1986; and European Year of the Environment 1987. Between them on an old brick wall is a PRAYER for PEACE:

'LEAD ME FROM DEATH
TO LIFE, FROM FALSEHOOD TO TRUTH
LEAD ME FROM DESPAIR
TO HOPE, FROM FEAR TO TRUST
LEAD ME FROM HATE
TO LOVE, FROM WAR TO PEACE
LET PEACE FILL OUR HEART,
OUR WORLD, OUR UNIVERSE.

PEACE

Cliff edge sign. © K. J. Varney

As you wander further along the Downs, almost next to where the lighthouse peeks into view, stands a plinth made of three descending concrete slabs. Just a couple of feet in height it is precariously placed on the coarse grass. On top is another plaque. Etched onto a dark background, the word of God shouts in white capital letters:

MIGHTIER
THAN THE THUNDERS
OF MANY WATERS,
MIGHTIER
THAN THE WAVES OF THE SEA,
THE LORD ON HIGH IS MIGHTY!
PSALM 93:4
GOD IS ALWAYS GREATER THAN ALL
OF OUR TROUBLES.

Mg

Mary Sisters' message. © K. J. Varney

Who is 'Mg' that has placed this permanent message so close to the edge? Luckily, Stuart McNab, who is familiar with every inch of the coastal path above and below, knows exactly how it got there. It is just one of 200 similar plaques located around British Isles, donated by the Evangelical Sisterhood of Mary. On their website, they praise the plaque for its spiritual power to prevent desolate people jumping from the cliffs:

Jumping spot. © K. J. Varney

Peace path. © R. Wassell

Mary Sisters. © The Mary Sisters

'If only praise plaques could speak, what stories could they tell us!'

They claim to have had one such story, reported to them by a lady in trouble, from this miraculous plinth at Beachy Head:

'I have suffered from bouts of depression for a number of years and...I went to Beachy Head fully intending to throw myself over the cliff. I was very drunk - I have had a drink problem for many years, too. As I was staggering along the top of the cliffs, totally out of my head - I literally fell over a plaque, which I hadn't noticed. I won't tell you what I thought of whoever had put it in such a stupid place! Anyhow, I got up and decided to see what it was all about and it read as follows.' She goes on to recite it word for word, concluding her story: 'It was as if something snapped inside me and I sat and cried like a baby - anyone seeing me must have thought I was totally insane! I suddenly thought of my children and knew I couldn't do that to them, however desperate I was, so I rang my minister from the top of Beachy Head...'

I was lucky that Stuart was on hand to tell me this information, but I was curious as to how this saved lady found out who had indeed placed the plaque that apparently stopped her from jumping over the edge that day. So I sent a message on their website. They apologised, explaining that they couldn't answer this question referring me back to the website. It was a little disturbing to then read their message to anyone accessing the website who may be feeling suicidal and turning to the Sisters' words for inspiration to carry on with life. It begins

Marking the peace path. © K. J. Varney

'Nothing to lose? A voice whispers subtly. It sounds smooth and pleasant, sympathetic and pitying. Many have heard it one time or another. "Put an end to it all! Then you'll be rid of your misery. It's the only way out. Life's a big let down. It hasn't given you what it promised. You've got nothing to lose." You really tried to get the most out of life and enjoy yourself. And what did it give you? Boredom, emptiness, despair, misery. You feel a wreck in body and soul. Why not put an end to it all? You're just a cosmic accident.'

Cross memorial. © K. J. Varney

If a suicidal person does manage to read on, it continues to tell of the damnation attached to running away from mistakes of your own making, and being in league with the prince of death, Satan; it ends by praising God in all his glory. Although well-intended the advice seems extreme and their messages confusing. The strangest of these is the supreme tribute of plaques the Mary Sisters have placed all around the world for celestial inspiration. They boast 'Praise plaques now mark many of the world's best-known scenic spots, from Kilimanjaro to the Swiss Alps, directing people to their Maker.' So if you don't trip over the message at Beachy Head sending you tumbling to your death, are you subliminally being shown the way to meet your maker?

Three separate memorials. © K. J. Varney

The memorials that speak a thousand words are the ones left by friends and family for those whom the plaques did not save. Some are tenderly cared for, others, while still poignant reminders, have dried in the southern sun. With every visit new posies or tributes appear. Eastbourne Council officials sometimes remove them, afraid of alarming tourists, but still the shrines appear as commemorations, moving the onlookers to mourn strangers, and stop for a moment's reflection. You watch as people creep closer to read the details; a laminated white card edged in black, hanging crudely from a tilting angle iron that no longer secures the thin wire fence meant to keep you from the crumbling terrain: 'Matthew Carson Casey Bennett 6 January 1982-20 July 2005. Beloved son, brother and friend'.

A sad memorial pinned on the fence. © K. J. Varney

Two wooden crosses placed at different times but in nearly the same spot; one has yellow pansies buried, barely flowering around the base, the other has red begonias with a gold plate simply stating: 'Michael 25.3.05'. Further along the wire, a tiny, bright-golden teddy bear is tied with string; its red mouth fixed in a strange sideways smile.

On two wooden posts, bouquets of pink roses and white carnations hang upside down wrapped onto the fence with a Tesco carrier bag pointing in the wind at a Remembrance Day crucifix and three red poppies.

A weathered wooden plank displays the message: 'Dangerous cliff erosion' etched in white, and attached to it is a bunch of dead heather. The sun shimmers on a wooden cross, the golden body of Jesus hanging in his suffering. Planted all around, pink roses lift their heads into the breeze and large chalk stones illuminate the scene, even in the dark of night, from the moon's glow. These commemorations are all terrible reminders of lives needlessly lost.

CHAPTER 5

The Selfless Vigilante: Keith Lane

'At Beachy Head in Sussex, a team of volunteer counsellors is on duty every evening. The scheme is run by a charity worker that was set up by a local man whose wife jumped to her death from the cliffs and is credited with having reduced the number of fatal jumps.'(endnote: Guidance to be taken at Suicide Hotspots. http://www.csip-plus.org.uk/RowanDocs/SuicideHotspots.pdf)

The man mentioned in the above government report is Keith Lane who did indeed set up the Maggie Lane Trust in honour of his late wife. Keith donates all monies earned from awards and donations to the Beachy Head Chaplaincy Team (BHCT) and other local mental health charities, but he has patrolled the headland alone without the help of a safety harness or God's divine intervention, and has been personally responsible for saving 29 despairing people, bringing them back to their families, or guiding them towards an institution that can help them.

But he takes no glory or gratitude from his achievements and asks for nothing apart from his own inner peace, and recognition from researchers and the government to accept that there is more to Beachy Head than meets the eye. Keith's wife is recorded as an 'accidental' statistic despite being reported as 'jumped to her death' in this report.

In the years after the police left the headland patrolling for would-be jumpers, the death toll has never ceased, the coastguards are now in charge and while they work tirelessly at sending out safety messages their main role is to search and rescue. No single civilian had patrolled the cliffs though in search of those most at risk of ending their lives at Beachy Head.

Then in 2004 the new redeemers arrived. The Beachy Head Chaplaincy Team began to patrol the cliffs. But there was also one man, Keith Lane, who patrolled alone: the new maverick on the cliffs. Keith is not part of the Beachy Head Chaplaincy Team, and he is not a member of the local church, but he has patrolled the headland every day since March 2004, in the early hours of daylight, and last thing at night, in an attempt to deter and befriend would-be suicidal jumpers. By day, he is an ordinary, 58-year-old, self-employed window cleaner with two daughters, grandchildren, and a new loving wife, Val, whom he met and married in 2006 after a whirlwind romance.

Keith has a sad personal story to tell. The death of Keith's wife in 2004 prompted him to begin a 'Charles Bronson' patrol on the headland, aiming to deter any potential jumpers. He is also unafraid to speak up about the despair of the many people he has met at the cliff top, who are moments from deciding between life and death.

Today it is bitterly cold, and the easterly wind whips at your clothes, threatening to push you closer to the edge, the sun is a mere glimmer on the far-off horizon. Keith stands with his back to the ocean, and welcomes you with a warm smile and gentle charm, hiding the anguish and sorrow that life has previously dealt him. He is, hauntingly, aware of the effects of suicide and the lethal consequences of taking that final step to infinity. In early March 2004 his, then beloved, wife, Maggie 'fell' to her death from the picturesque pike of Beachy Head. The memory of that day is painfully vivid to him. He left for work as usual early in the morning, kissing Maggie goodbye and promising to ring her later as he always did. Halfway through his rounds he recalls packing his ladder away, and calling her to make sure she was okay. She told him that she was fine. Confident that his wife seemed to be having a good day, Keith carried on cleaning windows in his local area. Little did he know that tragic events would unfold that would affect his life forever.

Sometime after that final call, Maggie, alone in the house, began drinking. Then she put on her make-up, styled her blonde, bobbed hair, and slipped on a pair of high heels. Dressed as if for an evening out she left the house, heading for the cliffs.

The grassy terrain and cold March winds do not make for easy walking on the cliff top, and high heels would make it doubly difficult. Perhaps it was a tragic accident, no one saw her fall. But, nevertheless, Maggie Lane perished that day, by stepping off the world.

Keith was told by the coroner that Maggie must have slipped because of the injuries she sustained to her left side, which where inconsistent with direct evidence of other fallers and recorded an open verdict. But he has other thoughts. He doesn't know why, but he is adamant that Maggie knew exactly what she was going to do.

With Beachy Head just a short drive away Keith talks about how he often walked along the Downs: 'It just doesn't make any sense. I've always come here, summer and winter, just to lose myself in the views, but Maggie, she would rarely come because she was so terrified of heights.'

It is part of the unanswered mystery of why Maggie chose to go to the cliffs that fateful day. He admits that he loved Maggie with a passion but life with her was not always easy. She had a long history of depression and alcohol abuse and on a number of occasions had attempted to take her own life at their Eastbourne home. A dark shadow crosses Keith's face as he relates the incident that took place just the week before her death. After an evening in, watching telly as usual, she had quietly gone upstairs and locked herself in their bathroom. When Keith checked on her minutes later, she became distressed, screaming threats through the wooden door that she was going to kill herself. Keith frantically tried to get her to open up, but Maggie simply ignored his pleas. So he ran around to the back of the house, and climbed up his work ladder, forcing open the small bathroom window. Peering in through the tiny opening, he saw Maggie slumped naked in the bath. He tried calling to her but she didn't respond. Wrenching the window fully open, he squeezed through the gap, reaching her just in time to stop her sinking slowly beneath the water. Maggie slowly recovered and sobered; holding her in his arms they gently made love. Afterwards, as they talked into the night, she told him how she had been having dreams lately that they had 'jumped over the cliff hand in hand.' Keith found this disturbing but thought no more of it when Maggie seemed to recover from the incident, slipping back into daily routine.

(endnote Suicide rescue 'sign from wife'
http://news.bbc.co.uk/archives)

Keith took the call that we all pray never comes. Breaking the sad news to his family was one of the hardest things he has ever done. They all tried, desperately, to help each other but Keith was wracked with grief, returning again and again to the cliff top, trying to make sense of why Maggie had gone onto Beachy Head that day.

In the days that followed, Keith began to experience the classic symptoms of suicide bereavement, as discussed in the comprehensive study by Hawton and Kees van Heeringen, (endnote: *The International Handbook of Suicide and Attempted Suicide*) 'that it is a common reaction to suffer in the aftermath with suicidal thoughts and could be part of a wish to rejoin the deceased spurred by a need to resolve unfinished business or may be induced by depression.'

Late one evening, he sat on the edge of the perilous cliffs, in the exact spot that Maggie had gone over, contemplating joining his wife in the afterlife. There were no trumpets, angels or mystic tempters by his side, but someone spotted him, and did raise the alarm. The police arrived to find him inconsolable; as he was so near the edge, they scuffled him, physically, to a waiting police car. He was taken into custody for his own protection and left in a cell overnight; he claims he was never offered counselling or any form of aftercare.

Keith has no previous record as psychotic, nor has he ever suffered from depression, abused drugs, been unemployed, or displayed any other suicidal tendencies whatsoever. He was a carer for his alcoholic wife who had, on five previous occasions, tried to commit suicide. With a feeling of torment and injustice suffered through this experience with the authorities when he was so in despair he made a personal vow to tame the beast that terrorises the cliffs of Beachy Head.

Since his release from custody, Keith has patrolled and campaigned to promote a transparent, open and robust investigation into the real statistics at Beachy Head on how deaths are recorded as opposed to open and narrative verdicts which aim to reflect a decrease in suicide rates at this challenging place. He is on a genuine humanitarian quest to implement a regime that offers sympathetic care, reassurance and support to anyone before they reach their perceived point of no return.

Keith and Val Lane. © K. J. Varney

His heroic acts to intercept would-be suicides are recorded, though not always reported, and in May 2004, having been nominated by the same Sussex Police that had previously incarcerated him; he received a Vellum award from the Royal Humane Society for preventing the suicide of a woman just one week after Maggie's death. It was Keith's very first brush with another desolate woman. Still suffering from shock and sorrow, he was wandering the headland at 5.30am on a misty March morning, when he spotted a lady crying softly. She was sitting on a memorial bench and appeared to be writing a last goodbye. He made eye contact and gently began edging his way over to talk to her:

'I hope you're not going to do what I think you are,' he said. But without warning, she shouted back:

'Leave me alone!' Jumping up from the bench she made a dash towards the sea. Keith called after her, with tears streaming down his face:

'I can't do that!' And proceeded to run after her. Just 15 ft from the edge, on pure instinct, he dived at her feet and rugby-tackled her to the ground. Keith

same sort of help as i. To get to that point you don't have to be some low life it can happen to anyone. Just remember that....'

There seems to be a real conflict over who should be on the cliffs to help those in need. The Beachy Head Chaplaincy Team have a close relationship with the coastguards and call on them if their own lives are put at risk and they need to be harnessed in order to talk a jumper down. But health and safety issues are not always the most popular rules to follow and certainly not met with any consistency by the powers-that-be.

In August 2007, the *Eastbourne Herald* told the story of a couple who won a police award for 'The dramatic cliff-top rescue' of a suicidal 13-year-old girl. Colin Stevens, a retired Metropolitan police officer in the child protection team and his wife, Barbara Stevens, a retired teacher, spotted a girl from their cliff top Newhaven home, sitting on the edge of the cliffs. It was a drizzly May day and she seemed forlorn and unhappy. Colin recalls: 'It was raining hard. I happened to be looking out of our window. We live on the cliffs and I saw this girl right on the edge of the cliff and looking very distressed. I got the binoculars out and called my wife over and said 'This girl's going to do something awful in a few minutes.' We went out and my wife was ahead of me and she went to speak to her. She knew she wanted to jump.'

His wife stood in the spring rain, talking to her until she agreed not to jump. The teenager went back with the couple to the safety of their house until police arrived and took her away for professional assessment. Chief Inspector, Peter Laverick, divisional commander for Lewes recommended Colin and Barbara for a bravery award, commenting: 'The officers at the scene were extremely impressed by the actions of Colin and Barbara Stevens. They probably saved the life of this young girl, whilst putting themselves at risk. Without hesitation I recommend this award.' The award was presented by Caroline Mayhew, the High Sheriff of East Sussex.

The couple's compassion cannot be criticised or lessened but there have been many instances where other 'heroes' have not received the same accolade for their bravery. On 12th January 2008, volunteer coastguard, Paul Waugh, aged 44, spoke of his treatment by the Maritime and Coastguard Agency that he had loyally served for 13 years. A year after a dramatic rescue of a 13-year-old girl, he has announced that he is quitting as a coastguard volunteer: 'I thought I would be a coastguard for life but I've been put under immense pressure. I couldn't carry on being treated so badly.' (endnote: Forced to quit for being a hero. Cliff rescue coastguard 'broke safety rules' the *Sun* pub 12/01/08)

It is not clear what treatment he received but his heroism is truly apparent. On a dark, January evening in 2006, above the wail of a storm force gale, he heard the tiny cry of 13-year-old, Faye Harrison, who was stranded 100 ft below on the crumbling Cleveland cliffs he usually patrolled. Without hesitation or the use of any safety equipment he scrambled down the rockface to reach her. For half an hour, he protected her from buffeting winds, restraining her from falling to the beach below until a dog walker spotted them and called 999. Soon the reassuring sound of an RAF helicopter arrived to rescue them both.

Locally, he was hailed a hero, receiving two awards for his bravery as it was the second time he had been a saviour to this girl. In 2006, when she was trapped by the tide on the shore below the cliffs, he had found her and taken her home to the safety of her family. Faye feels he is her 'Guardian Angel':

'If he hadn't been brave enough to climb down to me I don't think I would be here today. I was terrified and started thinking about my funeral,' (endnote: Hero coastguard quit in safety row. www.itv.com/News/Articles/archives)

A year on, life has become intolerable for Paul, and he decided to end his work as a volunteer for the coastguard agency: 'I broke a rule and did not use the kit but I saved a life. I don't call myself a hero. I would have helped even if I had not been a coastguard.'

The Maritime and Coastguard Agency (MCA) responded to Paul quitting with a statement: 'We wish Paul well in his future endeavours and the MCA is very grateful for his past activities and work in the Coastguard Rescue Service. However, the MCA is very mindful of health and safety regulations which are in place for very good reasons. Above all our responsibility is to maintain the health and welfare of those we sometimes ask to go out in difficult and challenging conditions to effect rescues. The MCA is not looking for dead heroes.'

In March 2008, Paul was honoured at a gala ceremony for the Children's Champions 2008 Awards with the 999 award for his bravery. Along with the other recipients he was hailed as 'an inspiration to the whole of the nation.' Keith has written a book about his story called *Life on the Edge* published by John Blake Publishing Ltd.

Keith still visits the cliffs but no longer to search for the most forlorn, he simply returns to the spot were Maggie perished to wish her peace and tell her he tried his best.

CHAPTER 6

Search and Rescue

For the steadfast 11-man team of volunteers of the Eastbourne Cliff Rescue Team, every time they descend the cliffs they put their own lives in danger. Generally their job is to recover a body, regardless of weather conditions, or sometimes a dog that has over-enthusiastically chased a ball or misread the distance from the edge.

Stuart McNab, is a calm, gentle, man who has dedicated over eighteen years of his life as a volunteer coastguard. As station officer for the cliff rescue team he explains:

'We have to make a rescue attempt for the dogs otherwise the owners try to do it themselves. Usually they're dead but in May 2006 a woman called us out because both her dogs had run over the edge. We winched down to recover them and when we reached them one of them was alive and well.'

Going over the edge to rescue the unfortunate is not for the faint-hearted. Once a call is received, the Dover Coastguard pages the team who then race to the scene, which takes, on average, 15 minutes. A four-wheel drive rescue vehicle and trailer carries a one-ton winch, a Larkin rescue frame, and 400-metre cliff ropes to anywhere along the cliffs. The triangular frame is hammered into the chalky ground with two hold-fast spikes to anchor it, which is unstable at the best of times. Once harnessed, and without any hesitation, over these brave saviours go.

Wrecked car wedged in a gully.
© H.M. Coastguard

Originally, it was the responsibility of the police then later the fire brigade to mount rescues and recoveries but, in October 1973, the focus fell on the coastguard which is now largely manned by over 3,500 volunteers countrywide. Despite modern safety gear the volunteers still get buffeted by winds which

Car in undergrowth. © K. J. Varney

force them against the jagged cliff face, where they are gashed on sharp flints that protrude from loosened chunks of disintegrating chalk, causing abrasions, bruises and, sometimes, fractured limbs.

In February 2004, two members of the cliff rescue team were winching a body up the cliff face when one of the rescuer's legs became trapped between the body and the crag, causing the lower part of his leg to be ripped, dislocating it from the top half, leaving him out of work for six weeks. It had proved to be a particularly busy week for the coastguards after four bodies had been discovered in just five days:

Climb back up. © H.M. Coastguard

'Rescue teams have been called out to Beachy Head five times this month - on February 1st, last Wednesday and Thursday, Sunday and Monday this week. The body of 31-year-old Lisa Parks from Lewisham, was to be found at the foot of the cliffs. Two further corpses were then recovered from Beachy Head on Wednesday and Thursday afternoon; just weeks after the remains of three others were found in one day at the same place. The body of Irene Lean, 53, of Rugby, was discovered east of Belle Tout lighthouse. But due to poor weather, rescue teams were unable to safely recover the body. A second corpse, that of Brian Fitzgerald, 53, of Tenterden Close, Eastbourne, was found while the Eastbourne and Birling Gap rescue team were at the foot of the cliffs. Coastguards then spotted another body on Sunday morning at around 11.30am after receiving a call from the public. And on Monday another corpse was discovered at the bottom of Beachy Head after a dog walker became concerned after finding a black rucksack.' (endnote: Four bodies over cliffs *Eastbourne Herald* published 11/02/04)

Cliff rescues are not the only duties carried out by the volunteers; they are on call 24 hours a day to respond to any type of incident as and when it occurs. Accidents can all too easily happen even on the calmest days. One man was seen falling to his death while he was leaning over the cliff to get a photo of

Coastguard and RNLI. © H.M. Coastguard

the lighthouse. When the coastguards reached him, his hand was still clutching his camera 500 ft down; his shattered body lay next to the dead body of a man who had gone over the cliffs undetected 24 hours earlier. A student also died when, walking close to the edge, the beers in his rucksack out-weighed him, dragging him over the edge before anyone could reach out and save him.

Similarly, two people in 2008 have been miraculously rescued alive. At 4.20pm on Saturday 29th March, Dover coastguards launched a full scale alert when a 47-year-old man apparently slipped on wet ground over the cliffs; he had fallen 80 ft landing on a narrow ledge but passers by still detected some movement. For the Eastbourne cliff rescue team the blustery March winds were perilous. Not only because

Coastguard. © H.M. Coastguard

Coastguards' hut. © K. J. Varney

the strong gales buffeted them against the cliff face but there was the added danger of the helicopter, hovering into the wind just 10 ft above their heads. Stuart McNab led the team. After making sure the winch men on top of the cliff had been anchored into the sodden ground to save being swept over the edge, Stuart descended the cliff. Calling on all his experience and instinct, to reach the injured man, as the terrible weather crackling into the microphone made communication erratic and distorted. Eventually the man was brought safely to the waiting ambulance with just a fractured collar bone and minor back injuries.

Then at 5.53pm on April 18th, 2008, as the weather was darkening the spring sky, and the sea was rousing rough with a south-easterly force 5-6 gale, both lifeboats were requested by Dover headquarters. The report involved a 16-year-old girl, who had gone over the cliff in the Falling Sands area; she was suffering from multiple injuries.

'The Inshore lifeboat with a crew of four was first on scene along with the Police helicopter H900. Two members of the crew went ashore and attempted to reach the casualty. After a number of attempts the crews were told to stand down and await further instructions. The All-weather boat with a crew of eight stood by just offshore and assisted with communications between the emergency services involved in the rescue. The casualty was eventually recovered by a joint effort of the local coastguard and the coastguard helicopter, which transferred her to the Eastbourne General Hospital.'(endnote: Eastbourne RNLI/Callouts)

The latest news is that she is set to make a full recovery despite landing 300 ft down. She was charmed, definitely one of the lucky ones.

In 2005, a 38-year-old man was killed when he lost his footing whilst launching a kite for his small children. He had gone to the cliffs, a little further along the coast at Seaford, with his ex-wife, two sons, aged two and four, and his seven-year-old stepson. It was a mild September Sunday afternoon, and the air was unusually still so he was having trouble getting the kite into the air. A walker saw him and warned him that he was dangerously close to the cliff edge. At the inquest, the witness told the coroner:

'The kite dropped and he pulled on the kite string, took half a step back and he was gone.' The hiker could only watch as the man plummeted 150 ft down the cliff face with his arms in the air desperately trying to grab hold of something on the way down. One of his children was still holding onto the other end of the kite. By the time the paramedics reached the beach he was already dead. (Dad fell to his death while flying a kite *Eastbourne Herald* First published 08/04/05)

Of course, there is always the threat of nature to consider. In August 2003, one woman in her 20s had a miracle escape. She had been relaxing in the summer sunshine, dangling her legs over the cliff face, reading a book. As she stood up to leave, the ground gave way, tumbling her body down the ragged cliff face. Further along the cliff, 16 coastguards had been demonstrating rescue techniques in front of hundreds of people when they heard her terrified screams. For 90 minutes, the cliff rescue team battled to reach her, reassembling their rig by cutting deep into the crumbling chalk top. As the rescuer descended he could see her motionless body lying on a narrow 8 ft ledge, 150 ft down. When he finally got to her he found her distressed but still alive with two broken wrists and non life-threatening spinal injuries. She was then winched carefully back to safety. (endnote: *Eastbourne Herald* Miracle Escape! pub: 5/8/2003).

India Juliet coastguard helicopter. © H.M. Coastguard

A few years later Councillor Chris Conil issued a stark warning to visitors when on 10th May 2008, a family, on a day out kayaking, was devastated by a sudden rockfall. Chris Tofts, aged 48, and his wife decided to relax in the sun after a busy morning at sea. As they lay on the beach, several boulders suddenly came tumbling down the cliff face, pinning Chris to the shore. As his terrified wife dialled 999, Chris lay there with a fractured pelvis and a wide gash across his stomach. Chris, once safely in hospital, praised Newhaven lifeboat crews and the coastguard helicopter:

'I owe my life to the amazing speed, skill and dedication of the Newhaven lifeboat crew and the extraordinary skill of the coastguard helicopter who came within a whisker of the cliff to rescue me.' (endnote: *Eastbourne Herald* Warning over crumbling cliffs. Pub 21/05/08)

Later in May 2008, Charlotte Forbes, a victim of the receding cliff, raised funds for the emergency services by cycling from London to Eastbourne in three days.

She had gone to Beachy Head on a clammy August day in 2003. As she sat some distance away from the cliff edge she suddenly heard a loud crack, the earth rolled away from under her, plunging her 200 ft towards the beach below. She desperately grabbed at rocks to break her fall but was finally stopped from hurtling to the shore by an old abandoned fridge. She fractured her spine in three places and suffered from two broken wrists. Recovery was long and painful for Charlotte and it was five years before she felt fit enough to take on the cycle ride to thank her silent saviours at Beachy Head.

With the toll of incidents and deaths once again rising at Beachy Head, the challenges for the coming years will surely stretch and test the emergency services.

Dog recovered. © H.M. Coastguard

It is impossible to know whether those that die accidentally or others that choose to end their lives here, consider just how much they rely on the voluntary emergency services to return their battered remains for a dignified burial. The seven-second fall from the highest peak, hurtles the body at 76 mph to the shore below. Tad Friend, an American journalist published an article in the *New Yorker*, Letters from California section. (13 Oct 2003). He outlined in terrible detail the total devastation on a body that has fallen from a height. It takes just four seconds to hit the ground or sea from this famous 220 ft bridge with a force of fifteen thousand pounds per square inch. 'Eighty five per cent of them suffer broken ribs, which rip inward and tear through the spleen, the lungs and the heart. Vertebrae snap, and the liver often ruptures.' Marin state coastguard, Ron Wilton, told him: 'It's as if someone took an eggbeater to the organs of the body and ground everything up.' (endnote: *The New Yorker* Letters from California. Jumpers. The fatal grandeur of the Golden Gate Bridge. Pub 13/10/2003).

Many men and women in the voluntary search-and-rescue services give up their free time to protect this famous beauty spot on the south coast of England, blending into the local community until called upon to face the ugliness of death. Their job is dangerous and has been known to be fatal. Back in 1979, the coastguard in charge and a police constable descended the cliffs on rope ladders, to recover the body of a 52-year-old man. Visibility was poor because of low clouds and the gusty winds so ferocious that the constable was blown on to the beach below, he survived with cuts and bruises. This was in the days of rigging and pulleys rather than the modern rescue aids we see today. It wasn't until the 1980s that there was helicopter back up for the coastguards.

However, even nowadays, no amount of high-tech equipment will guarantee their safety.

On Bank Holiday Monday in August 2008 Beachy Head was, as usual, bustling with walkers despite the overcast weather. By 4.30 that afternoon a double tragedy had occurred that would put all the rescuers in peril. The police helicopter had spotted a body 400ft down the cliff, the coastguards were alerted and David Nott of the Eastbourne Cliff Rescue team was tasked with being lowered to recover the body. Just as he reached the man he heard a commotion and as he looked back up the cliff face he saw a car come hurtling past him crashing onto its roof into the shallow waters. Stuart McNab was on the headland supervising the rescue, and was on his way to

Pensive consideration. © H.M. Coastguard

collect more equipment in their Land Rover when they suddenly spotted a red Toyota 4x4 mounting the grassy verge and heading for the cliff edge:

'I was in the passenger seat of our vehicle with Tony driving and Andy in the back.' Stuart could clearly see that it was an elderly man and at first thought he was lost. 'Then it dawned on us and I urged Tony to cut him off with our vehicle. He shot off along the cliff top. We put on our sirens to indicate for him to stop but he just sped up.' Suddenly he turned the car towards the sea plunging over the cliff edge. By now other teams were arriving; the police, inshore and offshore lifeboats, Birling Gap and Newhaven cliff rescue teams. A simple recovery had quickly become a major incident. While the offshore lifeboat remained in deeper water the inshore crews tried to reach the car to see if the man was still alive. Heavy surf made it difficult and treacherous. The police helicopter with paramedics on board swooped above watching as two of the lifeboat men took to the water desperately trying to swim against the tide. One of the volunteers, as he reached the shore, was thrown against the rocks injuring his shoulder. The coastguard helicopter had also arrived and after dramatic rescues the two lifeboat men, David Nott and both casualties were winched back on to the headland. The whole incident took seven hours. It was the dark of night before these brave volunteers reached home. The first man has not been publicly identified. The driver of the car was 77-year-old Geoffrey Monk who had made that solemn journey that day from his home in Oxfordshire.

Preparing to go over the cliff. © H.M. Coastguard

Talking to them about their work, each of them, from whichever branch of the services, seem reluctant to consider what they do as anything other than ordinary or necessary, recounting their experiences as what they term 'jobs' or 'shouts' with a modest dignity. But their roles are extraordinary in many ways. They need to have specialist skills and knowledge, and have to practise in inclement conditions, periods when the town folk and villagers alike are relaxing after a long day's work, as well as being able to cope emotionally with the terrible trauma. Central to all coastguard rescues are the sea-readiness of lifeboat crews that man vessels around all of Britain's unpredictable coastline.

The lifeboat station in Eastbourne has a long history in East Sussex; it was established in 1822, two years before the Royal National Lifeboat Institute (RNLI) was founded. 'Mad' Jack Fuller, who had also commissioned the first lighthouse on the headland in 1828, tenaciously set about establishing a sea rescue boat in response to a shipwreck near Beachy Head, involving 140 crew where six had died.

Within just six months, he had acquired and manned a 25 ft vessel, which he bequeathed to the people of Eastbourne after his death in 1833. It was originally moored at an old wooden boathouse on Marine Road. Later, under the command of the RNLI, conditions for the crews were substantially improved when it was moved to the Wish Tower in 1898, now the site of the Lifeboat Museum. In 1995, all operations were relocated to Sovereign Harbour Marina, a contemporary complex of stylish new housing and coffee bars, overlooking a bay full of weekend pastime sailing boats and dinghies, splendidly flanked by the familiar orange and blue iconic life-saving vessels. (endnote:http://eastbournernli.org.uk/Stationhistory.html)

Mark Sawyer is a long-standing lifeboat training coordinator and Coxswain for the RNLI, serving at Eastbourne. In 2003, he was awarded the RNLI's prestigious 'Silver Medal for Gallantry'. Sitting next to him in the new boathouse is Dave Needham, Senior Inshore Lifeboat Helmsman, with over 20 years service. Almost speaking as one, they nod their heads in agreement as they recount a unique side of their work with professional stoicism, tinged with compassion:

'Usually when we are called out there's always a good chance that we will be saving people, you know, those that have got into trouble at sea for whatever reason. That's really rewarding, even when it's been a battle to reach them through bad weather or rough seas. But recovering bodies at Beachy Head, that is a really difficult side to the job. As the lifeboat is activated you have to prepare yourself for any gruesome sight and the physical task of retrieving people that have been smashed onto the beach. But, when you get there you have to focus on not letting it affect you, reminding yourself that you are just recovering another body from the bottom of the cliffs yet you can't help thinking of the families they have left behind.'

The daily acts of bravery, saving lives at sea, marred only by this now routine job of recovering crumpled, broken bodies. Eastbourne lifeboat station is one of the busiest in the country, responding to an average of 100 call-outs a year; all the crews are only too aware that this high number is down to the desperate people, who come from the far ends of the earth, to Beachy Head with the sole intention of ending their lives.

Mark's expression suddenly changes to a more sombre one, as he reveals his fear, not of the flashbacks that he sometimes experiences, but the tangible panic he feels when he walks on the Downs:

'The cliffs have a magnetic almost magical energy that seems to draw you close to the edge, but I just can't do it. Walking on the cliff top is breathtaking and yet I can only get so close to the edge before I have to drop to my knees and slowly inch forwards.' Maybe the stark reality of the fall to the shore is too engraved on his mind having spent years scraping up bodies.

These quiet, gallant volunteers of the cliff rescue teams and lifeboats prefer not to be seen or heard except in our darkest moments of need and take no glory in their incredible work at this enchanting place.

Beachy Head for all its beauty truly has an invisible history. Smugglers, wreckers, watchmen and wanderers have all perished here, their memories scattered in the archives, untold stories of real lives, leaving behind a headland sprinkled with forgotten tears.

CHAPTER 7

The Lone Ranger

As you walk along the headland, heartbreaking memorials to the dead are solemn reminders all along the cliff edge. From the latest one, a plinth, laid by the Sussex Peace Alliance on May 24th 2008, commemorating all those who lost their lives in all the wars of the last hundred years, to the personal, tiny floral tributes left in remembrance of those who have ended their lives at the foot of the cliffs.

There is one, though, that sits alone, nestled in the downy grassland attached to a small wall that was once the Watch Tower from which Lloyds staff would watch shipping as it sailed the south coast. It is a carved picture of a policeman on horseback, with the following words etched into its brass face:

In memory
Of
P.C. Harry Ward
B.E.M. E.R.D.
1912 - 1974
The Downs Ranger
who patrolled Beachy Head
on his horse for many
years before retiring in 1966.
On numerous occasions he
risked his life attempting
to save others.

Harry's plaque. © K. J. Varney

In the 21st century, the new Downs Ranger at Beachy Head is a civilian who drives across the South Downs in a 4x4, tending to the farm holders and surrounding countryside. He no longer has the responsibility of the cliffs. But back in PC Harry Ward's day, things were very different. I was intrigued to find out more about this lone ranger. The local community was keen to help, through appeals in the local paper; I was able to find his family who pieced together an inspiring story.

Harry was a hero of a unique kind. Born in 1912, at the tender age of 13 he left school to join the railways in his native Blackburn. After three years he was sacked along with many other workers during a slump in the industrial north, so, at just 16, he signed up for the British Army. After basic training he was enrolled in the Household Cavalry as a Trooper, and soon became an accomplished soldier and horseman.

Having served for eight years in one of the country's most respected regiments he was at a loss as to what to do next. His dad was a policeman so he had earlier made a promise to himself that he would never follow in his footsteps, leaving his family for long hours with the torment of stress, and contemplated instead joining the Fire Service. But on a sunny August afternoon, while on a day out at the seaside on the Eastbourne coast, he made a decision that would change his life forever. In that summer of 1936, having just married Phyllis at Birmingham Registry office, for unknown reasons he suddenly made his mind up that he would, indeed, join the police force. So, moving his family to the sunshine coast he began his duty, serving the public as a traffic cop.

When Hitler marched his army into Poland, declaring the start of World War II, Harry was plucked from the reserves and once again called up for army duty. Starting in the military police in 1940 he was soon transferred to the Royal Artillery, joining the thousands of brave men at Dunkirk; his job was to lay booby traps for the enemy, to protect the British troops as they were retreating.

As he was leaving France, a gardener from the War Graves team had been hanging around the port talking to returning troops when he met Harry and begged him to take his son back to England with him. The first boat they boarded was dramatically sunk but Harry, fulfilling his promise, implored the captain of another ship to give them safe passage. The boy was safely passed on to the local authorities when they docked in England.

At home, Phyllis knew none of this and was fretting. Tenderly packed parcels she had sent to Harry had been returned, with: 'Unable to Trace' stamped in bold letters across the crumpled brown paper packaging. From her Eastbourne home she could hear the dreaded guns firing over the Channel. Then a telegram arrived one week after Dunkirk; fearing the worst she sat in her kitchen, refusing to open it.

Finally she knew she had to read it; to her joy it simply said: 'Meet me at the station.' Her brave young husband arrived at Devizes station in a brand new 'demob' suit. But his time in the forces wasn't quite over. He was put in charge of the guns on the east coast before ending his service as a Captain serving in Cairo. Having survived six years he was finally discharged in 1946.

As the world began to return back to normal he, too, went back to his old life in Eastbourne, rejoining the local County Borough police force. For the next

Harry Ward, Jumbo and Patricia. Photo by permission of the family of Harry Ward

seven years he patrolled the streets keeping law and order, but was occasionally drafted in to patrol the cliffs of Beachy Head, on a handsome bay horse, Princess Patricia, when the then Downs Ranger PC Henry Poole was off duty. This was another life-changing moment for Harry- it was now 1953:

'I happened to be on relief duty when I was asked. It was a beautiful day and I rode across the Downs in the sunshine, away from all the traffic and sound of the police radio and I thought then it was the life for me, to be my own boss and so on....Just the job for an old soldier.' Harry Ward was just 41.

To the visitors at Beachy Head, he was a local attraction; children would rush to stroke the horse, looking up in awe at the tall, handsome policeman on horseback. Each year together they would lead the Eastbourne Carnival. But most of the time this was a lonely patrol, especially in the winter months when the cliffs were almost deserted, and it wasn't long before Harry saw the other tragic side to the job. When Henry Poole retired, Harry took on the permanent post, but a few weeks later, he came face to face with his first experience of the deadly cliffs. As he was patrolling the Downs he noticed a crowd of people peering over one point of the cliff. Someone had seen a woman jump; Harry dismounted and also peered over the long drop. He could see what looked like a discarded puppet lying hundreds of feet below. He called on the cliff rescue team but, strangely, they were all off duty. Harry was the only person around who had been lowered over the cliffs in a few practice sessions and knew it was up to him to make the descent:

'I was scared to death. But I was lumbered. I had to go. There was no one else around and there was just a chance that the woman was still alive,' Harry told others afterwards.

By now more police officers had arrived and were wheeling out a 700 ft long reel of wire on a hand-cranked drum. Stuart McNab, the current station officer of the cliff rescue team, still has the equipment first used by Harry and describes it in scary detail:

Harry Ward cliff descent.
Photo by permission of the family of Harry Ward

'The piece that goes around the rescuer's waist is like a horse's girdle, all leather and about two foot wide. Sewn into it are buckles and rings which were used to tie a Hessian rope through and then attached to the drum.'

After over 18 loyal years, and many, many descents, Stuart still shudders at the thought of using this kit to make a recovery. But at the time it was all they had; these were pioneering days of cliff rescue. Harry wore a tin hat with a wide brim to protect his head; his police uniform shirtsleeves rolled up above his elbows; leather gloves for grip with his watch facing inward; and his ordinary working shoes. Still wearing his tie, Harry took the collapsible canvas stretcher and poles and a cumbersome field radio, attached also by cables to the clifftop, and made his first rescue attempt.

The first few feet down were the worst. Immediately, the wire cable began to dislodge lumps of chalk as he braced his feet against the cliff face. But he went on, slowly walking backwards down the sheer white wall to where the body lay. Looking up he could barely see the faces of his colleagues, and they soon disappeared from view. After what seemed to him like hours he reached the woman who had already died from her injuries. Strapping her lifeless body into the stretcher, he slowly began the long haul back up to the cliff top. When he reached the top, he was shaking from the effort, and admitted he had been 'damned scared.'

During his thirteen years as Downs Ranger, Harry Ward made over 30 descents like this. One of his daughters, Judi Johnson, remembers hanging around her dad while he was on duty:

'I loved being up there with him, though I expect I was probably in the way. I don't ever recall him missing a day's work, even when there was heavy snow, the type we rarely seem to get any more, where it stacked up high over the hedges, and all the roads would be cut off, he would walk all the way to cliff top to make sure the horse was okay. He hardly ever talked about the rescues but I do remember on one occasion he was really upset. He had gone over the cliff to rescue a woman, when he reached her she was still alive. He kept talking to her the whole time, trying to comfort and reassure her, he managed to get her to the top still conscious. She was taken away by ambulance but sadly died the next day. I tell you one thing that made him mad was the old telephone he had to use, nearly every time he went over, as he got bumped around, it would cut out and he'd be dangling there with no communication.'

It's easy to see why the antiquated phone made him so mad; the job was nerve-wracking and exhausting enough, without having to deal with the difficulties of archaic apparatus. The phone was a clumsy handset that had to be carried in a canvas bag on Harry's back which he had to fish out any time he needed to get in touch with the men on the cliff top in charge of hauling him and a body, back up the cliff. It was coiled on a portable reel and the cable was lowered with him alongside the rescue cable and would often hang in big loops, snagging on chalk or grass verges so as he was pulled back to the top the cable would be pulling him back down:

'The inevitable result was that the telephone cable parted with a great "twang" and there you are again - on your own, and the worse part was that you couldn't stop the blokes at the top hauling you up, even when it meant being dragged over a damned great chunk of chalk outcrop.'

It was also unreliable: 'Nearly always, the result was that you were six or ten feet past the spot where you needed to stop before you got through.'

On one occasion, Harry was sent to investigate a car that had gone over the cliffs, and was lying smashed on the beach. It was quicker to make a descent than to walk along the shoreline so Harry was lowered down in the middle of a howling snow blizzard. When he reached the wreckage, he suddenly realised that, once again, the radio was not working. Unable to tell the winch team on the cliff where he was, he began the long, hazardous walk along the shoreline to Birling Gap where he used a public phone box to report his position.

Harry grew weary of trying to manage with the old telephone so he began an unrelenting campaign to get a modern, reliable replacement. Eventually, the new kit arrived. It wasn't exactly the slim handheld that the police have today but, nevertheless, it was a safer two-way backpack valve radio with headphones.

Not all of Harry's work involved recovering bodies; he was often known to prevent the most wretched souls from jumping. His daily patrol was split in half. In the early morning before many of the visitors arrived, he would mount Princess Patricia and they would walk the beat together. After lunch he would stroll on foot among the tourists ever alert to those that were there for more sinister reasons. Originally the stable was a simple Nissen hut, a military shelter of semicircular cross section made of a corrugated steel sheet, built next to one isolated bungalow.

Later, opposite what was then the Beachy Head Hotel before it was burnt down in 1966, a tiny sub-police station with a stable attached was built. It was here Harry would bring those in distress; they would either be people he had found wandering forlornly on the cliffs, or spotted by the bus drivers. When the drivers saw someone acting suspiciously, they would stop the bus, phone Harry and he would ride gallantly across the Downs to meet them. A chat and a cup of tea generally seemed to do be just the medicine they needed to make the journey safely home again.

Another side of the job was to care for his horse. Although Harry had worked with horses many times throughout his career he wasn't a man to get sentimental about them. He did admit, though, that he had never realised just how much he used to talk to them,

'Until one day there was an explosion at the radar station which used to be right next to the stable. The place was hit by lightning and the whole lot went up with a tremendous bang. Poor old Jumbo (Princess Patricia's replacement when she was retired) was knocked all over the place but she recovered - except that she was totally deaf for a month or so. I found that out when I went up to feed her next day and she did not respond to the rattle of the feed bucket. But it wasn't until I took her for a gallop across the Downs that I realised how much she relied on me talking to her. When I reigned her in she would not stop and I had to tug damned hard to get her to a halt. It was then I realised that I had always told her to stop, or to go on and so on. After that, I had to retrain her to respond to a pat on the neck when I wanted her to stop.'

Another daughter of Harry's, Hazel Simons, recalls what happened just before Princess Patricia was put out to pasture in 1963. Harry had taken annual leave and while he was off, the horse lay down in the stable, stubbornly refusing to get up:

'Nothing could be done to get her on her feet until they called dad to get him to try. They were talking of hauling her out using a Land Rover, but dad went up to the stable door, looked over and said "Hello Pat, what are you doing down there?" Amazingly she got up!'

Not long afterwards, Harry and Jumbo met. Jumbo was an imposing 17-hand dapple grey Irish hunter, known well for her feisty personality. Harry Gape, a retired police commissioner who served 30 years with the Eastbourne police remembers:

'I had my own parking spot at the main station in Grove Road and sometimes Jumbo would be brought down. The ranger would leave him tied up in the garage and whenever I tried to get past him he would try and bite off the silver buttons on my uniform.'

Hazel also remembers that Jumbo wasn't fond of people and let them know it:

'She was a different kettle of fish altogether. An unpredictable character, she would try to bite the public, shy at a dropped cigarette packet and disgraced herself by charging through the local hunt to lead the way. That day she went back to the stable in disgrace.'

Judi also has some stories:

'Up at the stable you had to be really careful where you left the spade after mucking out. If Jumbo could reach it she would grip the handle in her teeth, and begin swinging it to and fro until she had built up enough momentum and let it go at the nearest person to her.'

Ray Woolston was the last Ranger to ever ride Jumbo. After joining Eastbourne police in 1967 he, too, became relief Ranger to PC Jack Williams, who had, in turn, taken on the role after Harry retired in 1966. By 1971, Ray and Jumbo were a familiar sight on the headland. On occasions, Ray would have to patrol on foot as rain, gales and low-lying cloud blurred the edge of the cliffs, making it too dangerous for the horse. Jumbo was older, but it seems as if she hadn't exactly mellowed:

'Jumbo could be very cantankerous at times. I can remember one incident on the head when a film crew was filming on top and I was on patrol and on my return to the police box I decided to take a look at what they were doing. I rode the horse up to near they were filming which was quite close to the edge of a steep slope and bearing in mind when sitting on a horse, I am about seven or eight feet above the ground, Jumbo started to walk backwards towards the steep slope and no matter what I did I could not stop her walking backwards. This then became very serious and dangerous so the only thing to do was dismount and walk the horse back to the box. Good job they weren't filming me as it was very embarrassing.'

In 1973, while out on routine patrol, 'Jumbo accidentally put her foot in a rabbit hole and stumbled. I got off the horse and walked her the short distance to the police box. The following day she was lame and so I contacted the vet who informed me that Jumbo had torn ligaments in her leg. She was never to recover sufficiently to be ridden again and was retired. I think she was 17 years old now and was put out to grass. A short time later she died and was never replaced with a horse on the Downs.'

Ray also has vivid memories of the dramatic descents he made over the cliff, more than 30 years ago. Standing on the verge of the precipice without any safety gear, he has an uneasy feeling about the mystifying power of Beachy Head:

'I do believe that when you stand very close to the edge there does seem to be a strange pull towards the edge and one has to be very careful not to be pulled over.'

Even with a full harness on Ray still found it somewhat of an ordeal:

'One tends to forget the dangers at the time and just get on with the job. I thought the worst time was at the very edge of the cliff when you are standing right on the edge just prior to going over. When you looked down to where you were going, it really looked a very long way down and the butterflies started but when you had been lowered several feet down then you had to concentrate on what and where you were going. The cliff face was not very stable in parts and you had to be careful not to disturb too much chalk. I can remember one person that I recovered and that was a woman, I think she came from Surrey. The bodies are not in a very nice condition as nearly all their bones are broken and they feel like jelly, but it is the police who have to try to identify that person right through to the coroners' court.

In these times Beachy Head lighthouse was manned and the keepers would notify police of any bodies that they could see from the lighthouse.

'The training consisted of throwing a rather large and heavy dummy over the edge and the policeman who had volunteered to be lowered would commence the descent. The policeman would be dressed in a boiler suit, heavy duty boots and wear a tin hat. I also wore shin pads to protect my shins from any falling debris. The person being lowered would be strapped in a harness that was then attached to a steel wire that went through a piece of equipment that I can only describe as an 'A' frame. This frame was positioned at the edge of the cliff so that it protruded over the edge allowing the steel wire to pass through it. This would enable the climber to abseil up and down the cliff face. The wire was then attached to a winch situated on the front of a Land Rover type vehicle and this in turn anchored down with large spikes that had been driven into the ground behind the vehicle and chains were then put on the spikes. The climber was in radio contact with those on the top of the cliff and he would direct the operators to lower or raise him as required. The whole operation would sometimes take several hours from start to finish.

The frame Ray describes was the most modern at the time. Harry Ward had been known to go over the cliff with just a rope. This was the case when a terrier, happily chasing seagulls misjudged where he was, plunging three hundred feet over the cliff. Harry could see his little body stuck head first in a water gully; his legs wedged against the chalk and in danger of slipping the further two hundred feet to the shore below. Harry didn't usually risk his life for an animal but, on this occasion, the dog was obviously still alive and terrified. So down he went dangling on a rope. When he got to the dog, he scooped him up into a canvas sack and brought him back up to a very grateful owner. For this rescue he received an RSPCA Award.

Harry gave up using a rope when the rescue team at the top ran inland so fast in order to gather enough momentum to pull him back up the cliff that his whole body was scraped on the rough flint and chalk all the way up. Hazel remembers him coming home that day looking raw and painful, telling her that he felt 'like a piece of cheese being grated.' From then on, he always used a wire which was by far the safest lifeline.

This wasn't the only injury he suffered; Hazel also recalls that one year he descended so many times that he developed snow blindness, so bright were the dazzling white cliffs when the sun shone on them. He only found this out when he had to go to court to give evidence on an incident, but was unable to read his notes. He was immediately admitted to a London hospital where he stayed for six weeks.

By now, Harry had already seen an improvement in communications but was still unhappy with the cumbersome stretcher. It had proven to be difficult on many recoveries, hampered his efforts, and was a threat to his own safety. This was the case on one extremely tricky descent when a woman had fallen from the cliff top, landing on a steep, sloping ledge, hundreds of feet below:

'It was pouring with rain when he went down and he found it practically impossible to get the stretcher round the badly injured woman, without her or himself - or both - slithering off the outcrop and down onto the beach. Ward fought for two hours that Saturday afternoon to get a stretcher strapped around the woman, risking his own life in a brave attempt to save hers. In the end, however, it was all in vain. The woman was so badly hurt that the P.C. feared that tightening the straps around her would aggravate her injuries. For the first part of the ascent, he fastened only one strap round her and almost literally manhandled her up the cliff. When he reached the section where the chalk rose vertically, he had no option but to strap her firmly into the stretcher, and she died before he got her to the cliff top.

Frustrated by this, he set about redesigning the old-fashioned canvas and poles. He came up with the idea of placing rails under the canvas sheet, shaped almost like a sledge, to make the ascent smoother. This device is still the foremost piece of kit used today for cliff and mountain rescue.

Harry Ward medal award.
Photo by permission of the family of Harry Ward

In the 1964 New Year Honours List, PC Harry Ward was awarded the British Empire Medal to add to his RSPCA awards, and his Emergency Reserve Decoration. On 30th June that same year, the Duke of Norfolk pinned the medal to his chest in front of his proud family: wife, Phyllis, and daughters, Judi, Hazel and Verna, for his devotion to duty and pioneering efforts in the field of cliff rescue. Two years later, PC Harry Ward retired, moving with Phyllis away from the headland to a quiet village nestled deep in the Wiltshire countryside. It was here, in 1974, at the age of 62, this brave, gentle hero passed away. His family misses him dreadfully and, in 1999, was upset to find that there was no trace of the stable or his work on the headland at Beachy Head. So they designed a memorial plaque, commissioning a local man at Sells Green, a hamlet close to their Devizes home, to produce a fitting tribute from his tiny workshop at the end of his garden.

Many years previously Phyllis was moved by a Blue Peter appeal and rather than have Harry's medals languishing in a drawer she sent them, in good faith, to be melted down to raise money for charity. Somehow, they ended up in the hands of a dealer.

As the craftsman was putting the finishing touches, etching the words into the plaque, a man happened to call on the studio. To everyone's surprise he suddenly exclaimed

"I've got that man's medals.' He had bought them from the dealer 15 years previously and kept them safe. The family was delighted to tell him the story behind his anonymous medals. He went on to exhibit them at the Towner Art Gallery in Eastbourne and happily joined the family at the unveiling of this now constant mark of distinction, forever remembered, finally at Beachy Head. And many do remember him. When the Mayor of Eastbourne, Beryl Healy, paid tribute to Harry, Hazel was touched by 'the people stopping on their walk to listen and I could hear people saying "I can remember him" which made it all worthwhile.' This was 34 years after Harry had hung up his police badge and saddle. (endnote: 1966 *Dark Blue for Courage* Wittle P The Angley Book Company Maidstone)

Betty Hollingdale remembers Harry well. With the sweet voice of a young girl that belies her 87 years, she has fond recollections of the Downs Ranger. As a young girl she would visit her aunt and uncle at the nearby Bullock Down Farm, spending many happy days playing on the headland. With the outbreak of war she left her factory job in London to begin training in Penzance as a Land Army girl. When her training was over, she was transferred to Eastbourne and was thrilled to do her duty on the family farm. It was there she met and married Charlie, a shepherd on the holding. They began their life together, moving into the bungalow, owned by Lloyds Shipping Company, perched alone high on the cliff next to the Nissen hut. Princess Patricia and the then Downs Ranger, Henry Poole, had been moved to the hut from Bullock Down Farm as well.

After the war, Betty found work at the Beachy Head Hotel while Charlie tended to the sheep on the Downs. They soon became used to the familiar figure of Harry Ward:

'He was such a kind but no-nonsense man. As we were the only house nearby, sometimes he would pop in, making sure me and Charlie were okay and stopping for a cup of tea.'

Often when their daughter, Jocelyn, came home from school, they would still be both at work, and she would sit on the wall watching, and chatting to, the friendly policeman. Betty chuckles:

'He was good like that. But he did give me a right ticking off one day. It was about 1960 and I was quite young, in my thirties, I think. It was a warm summer evening when someone came knocking on the door. He was frantic "A woman has just jumped" he shouted. Well, Charlie was still out and Harry was off duty so I ran to the phone and called 999. Then I ran over to the cliff edge. I looked over and I could see a woman lying on her tummy, about 25 foot down, desperately gripping onto tufts of grass to stop herself slipping further down the rock face. I can still picture her face now. There was nothing else for it, I dropped onto my bottom and slid down to her. When I reached her I suddenly thought "what have I done" I didn't dare look down. I looked up instead and a group of holidaymakers had gathered on the edge watching us. Then they began to join hands, making a human chain, I took the woman's hand firmly in mine and slowly we were pulled back to safety. The police and ambulance arrived, taking her off, so I wandered back towards my house, everyone else was starting to move on. But there at my front wall a man was standing, his face as white as the cliffs, I asked if he was okay. He surprised me when he said "That was my wife; I didn't know what to do. We've got an appointment tomorrow for a psychiatric assessment in London. I thought a day out would help her." Well I thought fancy bringing her here!'

As dusk fell over the Downs Charlie came home and Betty told him all about it. Normally a very quiet man he raged at his wife yelling at her that she must have been crazy, and made her promise never to do such a thing again. The police didn't give Betty such a stark warning when they visited later that evening to take her statement of events. Instead, they left her with a long reel of nylon rope for the next time she might carry out another rescue.

The next morning Harry had got wind of the dramatic rescue, before even tending to his horse he marched up to her little cottage and knocked heavily on her door. When she had finished telling him all that had happened, she remembers vividly

'He went mad at me, ooh I did get told off. As he left he lifted up the rope the police had left and walked straight out of the door with it.'

After nine happy years living at the edge of the world, Betty has since moved into a tied cottage back on her beloved Bullock Down Farm. Her son became a member of the Birling Gap cliff rescue team.

Harry retired from the police force in 1966, moving away from Eastbourne to a country cottage in Wiltshire. Sadly, just eight years later he passed away at the young age of 62.

Harry's story has rarely been told, maybe next time you visit Beachy Head take a walk over to his lasting memorial and tell others his valiant tale.

Historical footage of Harry Ward can be seen at:
http://www.britishpathe.com/record.php?id=146 Harry Ward police Downs Ranger.

CHAPTER 8

The Haunted Shore

So what is the view from the shore? Finding the answer to this question requires a tinge of morbid curiosity to encourage an exploration to the base of the cliffs and a rare view from the lighthouse back onto the Downs. The Eastbourne tourist board does not openly encourage visitors to take this journey, issuing safety advice for children and the infirm to keep to approved trails. So guidance comes from local boatmen who know only too well the daily idiosyncrasies of the tide. The advice is not to wander the seashore without heeding their stark warnings of the perils of the sea.

A flickering moment of hesitation enters your mind as the local boatman appears to twitch slightly at guiding you to such a risky, risqué place:

Bay. © K. J. Varney

'Head out to Cow Gap, arrive at low tide and be watchful as the sea will not hesitate to claim you as her own. Be there by 9.20 and don't stay longer than two hours.'

His tone is both cautiously Victorian and eerily austere. If you close your eyes his image conjures an old, bearded kind of crooked man, bronzed by the wind who has seen every wrath of the waves. His wise warnings are taken seriously as there are many stories of people who have perished unwillingly, from sailors to tourists, at this bay of beauty.

Just over a mile outside the bustle of Eastbourne there are no signs for Cow Gap, which is the nearest access to the beach below Beachy Head. The only option is to wait, patiently, for a local resident and ask the way. The locals are easily spotted by their brisk walking as opposed to the slow, easy pace of the holiday-maker. Offering a wary interest in the naive urban traveller, asking directions raises eyebrows:

'Are you sure? Well I hope you're prepared,' the local warns; 'it's a long, hard scramble.' They point the way and watch as you head off to the Downs.

Soon the pavement gives way to cobbled slabs and dry stone walls overhang with flowering cherry blossom trees. At the grassy verge of the steep incline up onto the South Downs is a tiny but full car park. Overspills of visitors' cars are parked at angles all along the narrow road that leads up to the headland. Walkers are already puffing their way up the first hills, leaning on seasoned walking aids, their rucksacks full of provisions for the long trek ahead. Nestled in the corner is a bustling café with awninged tables offering homemade cake and tea for those already on the descent. A left turn here offers adventure to a much less trodden pathway. A wooden stake is styled like ancient graffiti, and crudely etched into are the words: 'Beachy Head 1¼ miles'. For a few hundred yards, the path is open, passing quaint cottages and other tourists but as it bends, a weather-beaten, wooden 'Cliff edge' warning sign turns many people back.

Beachy Head sign. © K. J. Varney

Gorse bushes overhang the pebbly path and the easterly wind begins to bite. The climb rises and drops as the trail narrows, embraced by the flora. Tiny, pale blue, common butterflies dance on the hedgerow. Rabbits dart in front of the path catching you unaware. The view is dramatic with sheer drops to the left and expanses of green fields to the right; families and dog walkers strolling in the spring sunshine becoming smaller and less defined. Rickety wooden steps missed or ignored by health and safety lure you further towards the beach. The going is tougher now; sliding down the crumbling cliff face, rough flint and jagged soft rock strew the earth below your feet, making it unstable and hazardous.

Adonis blue butterflies. © K. J. Varney

The lifeboat crews are called out on many occasions to this isolated beach to rescue people either trapped by the tide or suffering from fractured limbs as a result of the precarious journey up and down to the shore. This was the unfortunate case for a man on the 7th October 2007. On an unusually sunny winter morning a walker on the cliff edge heard a cry for help from the rocks below just west of the lighthouse. Receiving the emergency call, the Dover Coastguard dispatched a lifeboat at 11.52am to Beachy Head. They found an exhausted man in his 50s who had made various failed attempts to save himself.

After taking a stroll along the beach, 'He found himself cut off by the rising tide. His mobile phone was not receiving any signal down under the cliffs, so he was unable to raise the alarm himself. He tried to light a signal fire by striking flint stones together, after this failed he attempted to construct a small raft from barrels and pieces of wood he found amongst the rocks. This also failed and he attempted to swim but the tide was too strong. Attempts to signal passing boats by tying his shirt to a piece of wood and using it as a signal also failed.'

Weary and embarrassed by his predicament, he gratefully climbed into the inshore lifeboat, where the crew took him to safety and made him a welcome cup of tea. (endnote: www.eastbournernli.org.uk/callouts2007.html)

Despite this difficult journey to the shore and all the perils it presents, it still captures the imagination and drives you on. Suddenly, the familiar red and white lantern peeps into view and the arduous trek has been worth it. In the

Beachy Head, difficult path to the shore. © K. J. Varney

distance the 100-million-year-old cliffs blaze with stunning whiteness and the sun-speckled sea ripples with serenity. A breathtaking, yet, poignantly tragic, haven of peace. The reality of a perfect view from the cliff top transforms; the sea no longer laps at the feet of the cliff, but sits waiting a mile out to return. At low tide the shingle is exposed as a less than hospitable boulder base. Large, immovable, green-coated rocks delay the journey to the lighthouse. Zig-zagging over the least lethal of them there is hardly time to reach it before the sea begins teasing you to turn back, lapping easily back to shore.

The sightseer, a mere pinprick over 500 ft above at the cliff edge, is a stark reminder that at any time they may tumble or jump onto your path. As you clamber over the slimy boulders a change occurs; a tiny bend reveals a pool of shimmering water filling a sandy bay, too isolated to be real, too alive to be a place of death. Chalk and flint pebbles lie black and white among the fossil sponges. Crabs share the space with human debris, barnacles clinging to rusty car shells. A reminder of what still remains long after man, time and tide have tried to remove. Stark, subtle testimonies litter the beach: discarded rope, shredded items of clothing, a single shoe, even parts of a car engine. You brace yourself for the fear of discovering a body or even a body part that the coastguards have missed.

Finding gruesome remains along the shore is not as unlikely as it sounds. In August 2007, John Foundling, his wife and two children were exploring the bay below the cliff. Just as they were heading for Cow Gap at 12.40pm to make their way back for lunch they discovered the body of 32-year-old Lesley Ann Francis. The Foundling family had travelled from their home in Hampshire to enjoy a summer's day together, but Lesley Ann had left her London home with a far more tragic intention. Suffering with post-natal depression she had been previously hospitalised for mental health problems on numerous occasions. Coroner Alan Craze said at her inquest:

'It is a possible suicide and many would say a probable suicide but it has to be proved beyond reasonable doubt. I do not have a note or text message which can often help me in cases like this - she does not seem to have said to anyone that she was liable to harm herself. For that reason I must record an open verdict.' (endnote: Mystery surrounds mum's cliff death. *Eastbourne Herald.* Pub: 07/04/08.)

Similarly, although many bodies are located on the shore within a day or so, this was not the case for one local woman. While Stuart McNab was on duty with his team early one chilly January morning, they came across the decomposed, skeletal remains of a woman. He later found out that she was the mother of a young girl he had previously worked with. She had been missing since the previous April and at some time during that long period of

Boulder bay. © K. J. Varney

nine months, had gone over the edge, landing in deep gorse bushes that could only be seen from the cliff face. If the fall hadn't killed her, exposure surely had.

Another body was discovered on a Sunday afternoon in 2005 while members of the Eastbourne cliff rescue team were on a routine search of the area. The partially decomposed body of a man from Essex was wedged on a ledge of undergrowth and scrub 450 ft down the cliffs. It took nine coastguards, six hours to winch his remains to the top of the headland. Stuart, who led the recovery, later commented:

'The Eastbourne team does a magnificent job in all weather conditions to recover casualties from the cliffs. Most are straightforward, however, on occasions we do find bodies that have lain undiscovered for some time. It means that because of the advanced stages of decomposing, it makes the recovery and conditions difficult and unpleasant for members of my team.' (endnote: Body found at Beachy Head Pub: 6/07/05 www.eastbournetoday.co.uk/archives)

Furthermore, at least one man is known to be buried under a large boulder, his remains left where they fell. He was identified as a 65-year-old Brighton man who had been missing for eight months by keys that had fallen from his pocket on the descent but his body was already so decomposed that only the edges of his rotting clothing were visible, trapped under 1500 tons of immovable rocks.

Car in water. © H.M. Coastguard

Down on the shore, it is strangely quiet, the silence only disturbed by the faint ripple of the waves in the far distance; the tiny shivers of dusty chalk falling from the cliffs seem to have a voice of their own. There are no boats on the horizon and not another living soul seems to be nearby. The lighthouse keepers no longer watch from the tower, a monument so stunning in its isolation.

Then a reality intrudes. At the very base of the cliffs the eerie loneliness of the landscape gives way to a surreal snapshot of human nature.

Oblivious or strangely voyeuristic to the devastation of this place, human life explores a very different lifestyle. For slightly higher, just above the tide line, is a naturist sanctuary, a place that does not feature on websites about known naturist spots, and appears to be a local secret, guarded by the regulars and protected by the remote, forbidding habitat.

Human limpets hang from the cliff. Sun-kissed naturists sit nestling on the jagged ledges. A disposable barbeque invades your other senses, the unmistakable smell of bacon. A middle-aged couple contentedly cook up a portable full English. They look over with a Devil-may-care attitude that stares at you as the invader, the spectacle. Suddenly you feel caged by the sea, the cliffs, and are overwhelmed by the unexpected sight you have unwittingly intruded upon. Stumbling upon a viable and uninhibited choice of lifestyle that beggars the question: Is this the place of all temptation? Scanning the cliff face you now notice more solitary people, dotted on rough ledges stark-naked, offering their vulnerability to a sublime closeness to a heavenly place. The trek back is less adventurous and more urgent. The soul is unsettled, trying to make sense of the disparities.

Naturists. © K. J. Varney

Pete Hurt is 52 years old and has been a naturist for as long as he can remember. On fine days, he spends his days off lounging, exposed to the elements on the cliff face, just above the line of samphire that cannot grow

View of the path. © K. J. Varney

under salt water, safe from the rising tide. He is a well-known local man who has worked for over 30 years for Allchorn boats on the beach, west of the Eastbourne pier. For the last 140 years, from early May through to September, Allchorn boats have been operating heritage pleasure boat cruises taking tourists on trips around the lighthouse. (endnote: www.allchornpleasureboats.co.uk) There is often a queue of excited visitors who are entertained by the easy banter of the crew. For 45 minutes the *Southern Queen* sails, hugging the shoreline past the Wish Tower, Holywell and Cow Gap, the deep green Sussex Downland blurring as she cruises towards the famous lighthouse.

As it comes into view the tower stands proud on huge granite blocks sliced together like jigsaw pieces that have been cut to perfect size in a Cornwall quarry. It is easy to see why it took two years to build the seven-storey building that rises towards the sky. The tide is in so the boat pulls almost alongside, allowing the passengers to see every detail of the 3,660 tons of granite that was lowered down the towering cliffs over 100 years ago.

Pete has the all-round look of a seafarer, weather-hardened and jolly as he recounts the history of every inch of the shoreline to Beachy Head along the way: tales of places such as Whitbread Hollow, nicknamed 'Frenchman's Hole' as it was the burial place for the invading French sailors who perished during the Battle of Beachy Head in 1690.

In the winter months the company of holiday makers is a memory to Pete. During the cold season he leads a more solitary life, repairing and restoring the boats in a large, chilly boathouse further along the coast. The corrugated roof is battered with torrential rain, and old wooden oars, never to be used again, hang from the stalls. Boat grease covers his once-blue overalls. Pete also enjoys the naturist beach by the cliffs and he talks easily about his desire to go back to nature. Not in the gay public arenas of sectioned-off Brighton or the tiny square at the edge of Holywell where voyeurs have been strolling since England's first sanctioned naturist beach opened in1979; but in the private, tranquil unknown ledges of the Beachy Head cliffs.

His tone is measured, not aiming to sensationalise:

'It's nicely erotic,' he says; 'it's not just locals. We show a mutual respect for anyone that chooses to bathe here, keeping a distance but offering silent recognition and encouragement to one another that their secret is safe. Do you know what I mean? A nod or a wink. Never gossiping or telling on each other no matter how high profile they are. We get all sorts. I have seen a peer of the realm with someone other's wife, a couple of MPs, a high ranking police officer, all safe in their anonymous skin.'

Steps. © R. Wassell

Pete is a seasoned seaman and is fully aware of the hazards of wandering the cliffs, clothed or unclothed, describing the place as brutally beautiful. Although the naturists make sure they stay above the tide line in tiny niches on the cliffs, they are aware that when danger threatens, modern technology often fails. Thus, Pete always carries distress flares and carefully chooses where he sits, usually out of the line of falling bodies, although even in the most carefully planned spot a naturist

Cliff bottom. © K. J. Varney

Sad evidence. © K. J. Varney

Wrecked car. © K. J. Varney

might still be at risk of embarrassment or danger.

On one occasion, Pete was peacefully sleeping in the mid-afternoon sun. When he opened his eyes he was startled to see four nuns with a group of children in front of him; he quickly covered up until they had left the beach. Another time he watched as a lifeboat searched for a dog that had gone over the cliffs at Belle Tout. Amazingly the dog was unhurt and he spotted the spaniel running on the shingle shore. He also remembers an incident on an April Monday morning when he was sitting against the rocks:

Shore. © K. J. Varney

'The place is so hypnotic you totally forget. I was sitting quietly when suddenly rocks came scuttering down. I jumped out of the way, away from the cliffs, then there was a clump. I was just west of Cow Cap where the area is craggy on the walk down to the shoreline. Right there in front of me was a young girl, she was grazed and bruised. I went to her, to check she was okay, in broken English and between sobs, she told me she was a 15-year-old Danish student, and she had tripped on the way down falling about 30 ft to the beach. The lifeboat came out, checked her over and took her back to the safety of her group.'

As you stand on the shingle, watching over the ocean it's easy to see why Pete loves this extraordinary cove. This tiny shoreline appears tranquil, the shimmering bay reflecting a dazzling whiteness from the chalk cliffs slowly created when a sub-tropical sea covered the area. Forming over a period of 30 million years from microscopic planktonic algae, hardening into layers of white rock a thousand feet thick before finally emerging from the sea as the ice melted in the oceans.

The easterly wind that bites so harshly over the headland is merely a whisper on the spring breeze. Allchorn pleasure boats, packed with day visitors, sail by, encircling the candy-striped lighthouse silently watching over the sea. Seagulls, sensing something, cry in chorus as they dive and swirl around the cliff top, disturbed from their nests. The coastguard helicopter appears on the horizon, breaking the silence, hovering like a wistful humming bird, searching out another crumpled cadaver.

This haunted shore for too long the keeper of man's dreadful suffering.

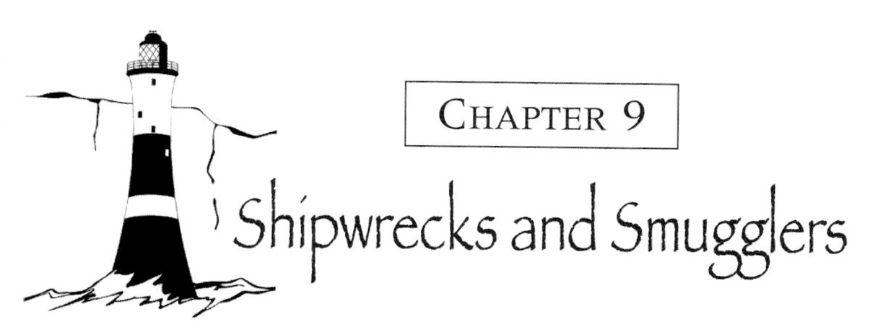

CHAPTER 9

Shipwrecks and Smugglers

Bella Bathurst in her book *The Wreckers* tells the true tale of Britain's unforgiving coast. She treads carefully on the dead souls of the 'wreckers', questioning whether they were merely lucky rather than a malicious bunch of rogues: 'Geography, weather conditions and a hostile sea washed up all the ships they would ever need. Though it is impossible to verify, probably rather less than one or two per cent of all British shipping casualties were ever actively wrecked by those onshore - mechanical failure, human error, navigational miscalculation, storm gale, lee shore - and were simply exploited by those who found them.'

It is thought that there are approximately 30,000 to 33,000 wrecks lying undisturbed at the bottom of British mainland shores. Some areas are more littered than others. A little way up the coast at Goodwin Sands it is estimated that there are an amazing 32 wrecks per mile.

Beachy Head. © R. Wassell

Around Beachy Head there are over 70 recorded wrecks, which is possibly a serious underestimate as in the past many ships were not registered, smaller vessels did not need to be and no doubt others floundered which were illegally sailing the seas with smugglers' booty. All too often there was evidence where bodies were washed up but with no sign of the stricken ship to record. Once a ship had run aground on the rough ledges or fast-flowing tide of Beachy Head, the cargo became fair game for local plunderers. But early British ruling meant a treacherous fate for the sailors who survived. Bella Bathurst explains how, in medieval times, all salt water matters were considered the responsibility of the English Crown, in the same way as were the soldiers and serfs, and all bounty was 'The packhorse of the King.' Therefore any goods washed up would automatically belong to the realm.

By 1236, ship owners, tired and impoverished by their losses at sea, protested to the Crown that their goods should remain their property even when it was washed up on the shores. King Henry III finally passed a charter that allowed the owner of wrecked goods to reclaim their bounty as long as it was within three months of the ship running aground. To ensure that disabled ships were salvageable or refloated and not deliberately seized and destroyed by locals, he included a bizarre clause: if any man or beast escaped alive from a ship then it could not be truly considered a wreck. The implications of this clause were devastating, and the legal loophole became a licence to murder. When a sailor was washed onto the beach close to death, his life was in the hands of the plunderers who quickly hastened his demise, either murdered or left to die on the shoreline, so they could legally claim the spoils. This clause remained on the statute books until 1771 when it was finally repealed.

Yet it persisted as common lore and was a continued practice in remote areas as late as the nineteenth century through to the early twentieth century. Articles were added which gave account of this terrible practice and sought to deter these murders but to no avail. In 1266, Article XXX 1 of the Rules of Oleron states: 'If a ship or other vessel happens to be lost by striking on some shore, and the mariners thinking to save their lives, reach the shore, in hope of help, and instead thereof it happens, as it often does, that in many places they meet with people more barbarous, cruel and inhuman than dogs, who to gain their monies, apparel, and other goods, do sometime murder and destroy these poor distressed seamen; in this case, the lord of that country ought to execute justice on such wretches, to punish them as well corporally as pecuniarily, to plunge them in the sea till they be half dead, and then to

Coastguard cottages. © R. Wassell

have them drawn forth out of the sea, and stoned to death.' (endnote: Bathurst B. (2005) *'The Wreckers'* Harper Collins London)

Postcard - Beachy Head.

One of the most famous wrecks at Beachy Head was the *Nympha Americana* on 29th November 1747 which was captured near Cadiz by Commodore George Walker, en route to London via Portsmouth. As she turned into Birling Gap cove she was smashed against the rocks, capsizing on the beach below the cliffs. All thirty of the crew perished on board. News soon spread of her rich cargo of fine velvets and materials, £5,000 in hard cash and £30,000 of quicksilver. The beach became swamped with people from far and wide who pillaged off all they could carry, though not without casualties. It is claimed that 60 more died on the shore through accident, having sampled too much of the on-board liquor, or through being shot for looting. It would take a separate research to determine exactly how many mariners perished on the shores of Beachy Head.

The Rye Castle Museum records: 'There is an exceptional shoreline concentration of historic shipwrecks that can be visited by non-divers at suitable low tides. It lies in East Sussex between Camber in the east and Cuckmere Haven, just west of Beachy Head in the west, where there are preserved the substantial remains of large ships of the seventeenth, eighteenth, nineteenth and twentieth centuries. This range of age for ships visible at low tide has no known parallel in Britain, and may be unique in Europe.' (endnote: http://www.ryemuseum.co.uk/archives)

In 1836, the last year of the 'sailor king' William IV's reign, a Shipwreck Committee was set up to investigate why so many ships had been floundering. Their early reports found that it wasn't just the unpredictable sandbanks, rocky coastline or heavy weather that were responsible. The shipping industry was beset with dishonest and unprofessional practices sanctioned from the docks all the way up to the corridors of Parliament.

Poorly maintained and unseaworthy merchant ships were allowed to go to sea to save the costs of repairing them. A political blind eye was turned when their cargo, more often than not, exceeded safety limits, overloading the holds to dangerous levels. Captains were appointed based on family tradition or influence rather than their seamanship. There are records that once there was a captain as young as 14, all of his crew were older than him. With the lack of navigational training, inadequate harbours, and inaccurate charts, it is hardly surprising that many ships and lives were lost around Britain's coast. Wreckers were replaced by plunderers who picked clean the hulls, and welcomed the gifts of the ocean.

But the main cause of shipwrecks according to the committee was the menace of rum: 'Drunkeness,' they stated, 'either in the masters, officers, or men, is a frequent cause of ships being wrecked...the practice of taking large quantities of ardent spirits as part of the stores of ships, whether in the Navy or in the Merchant Service, and the habitual use of such spirits, even when diluted with water, and in what is ordinarily considered the moderate quantity served to each man at sea, is itself a very frequent cause of the loss of ships and crews.'

The Maritime Marine Board was established to try and bring about a national code of practice. Recommendations included: regulations to be imposed regarding the design and construction of vessels; court hearings to examine the case of every ship that ran aground; the addition of life-saving devices on deck; attention to the habits of the sailors including hygiene; and the level of aftercare following a shipwreck. The board also advised that exams in 'seamanship, navigation and nautical astronomy' should be taken by future employees, and each sailor should wear a recognisable uniform. Finally the committee strongly recommended that all alcohol should be withheld, and to replace it with rations of tea, coffee or cocoa instead.

These are all things that seafarers now take for granted but, at the time, the ship owners were suspicious of government interference and reluctant to make any changes, even if they were for their own good. It wasn't until seven years later, having lost 240 British ships and 500 lives in the space of three years that the committee met once again to discuss the tragic and economic cost to Britain's place as a sea merchant power. This time the group looked into other means of protecting ships not so easily influenced by individual ship owners. These included: lighthouses, floating breakwaters, lifeboats, coastguards, rockets, and mortar. Once again, the welfare of the crew was examined including their wages, training, and on-board punishments.

The committee tried once more to ban the consumption of spirits whilst sailing the high seas. By the late 19th century a concession was made with the reduction of rations of rum but instead of replacing them with tea, coffee or cocoa as recommended the rum rations were replaced with gin. Such was the tradition and culture of sailors that it took until 1970 before all alcohol consumed on duty was banned by the Royal Navy.

The haunted shore, witness to sea battles, suicides and smugglers, has many

Shipwreck off Beachy Head. © R. Wassell

more tales to tell. In the 17th century and early part of the 18th century no organisation existed to prevent illegal goods being landed on the south coast of England, despite the Romans having the vision to watch the shores for invasions from Saxon longboats in 400 AD, and the Tudors creating watchers on the cliffs to warn of any attack from the Spanish Armada which paid off when the first sighting was dispatched to London via Beachy Head. Not only did the smugglers have a free hand at landing goods, they were also hard at work taking goods, such as valuable wool and tin across to Europe. Smugglers additionally, secretly, exported espionage services out of the country most notably to England's most sworn enemy: Emperor Napoleon Bonaparte.

As an exile in St Helena, after his defeat at the Battle of Waterloo in June 1815, Napoleon took pride in revealing that during his war campaigns much of the money he needed to pay for his military conflicts had been transferred from the City of London, by more than 500 smugglers. Money was laundered from Spain through London by merchants for a 10% fee and brought back to France, more often as gold. Napoleon states: 'They did great mischief to your Government. During the war all the information received from England came through smugglers. They are people who have courage and ability to do anything for money.' He continued his boast with: 'I had every information I wanted from them. They bought over newspapers and dispatches from the spies that we had in London. They took spies from France, landed and kept them in their safe houses for some days, dispersed them over the country and bought them back when wanted.'

In return for this invaluable service, rather then being mistreated as 'the enemy' when they were in France, the smugglers were given accommodation at Dunkirk. There they would load the ships with contraband to smuggle back into England. For many years smugglers maintained a good relationship with the coastal port of France.

In 1779, at a time when 50% to 65% of all spirits consumed in Britain were illegal imports, a distillery at Dunkirk gave over all its gin production to the smugglers which was brought ashore at Crow Link Gap, just west of Beachy Head. The ease with which they could land the goods tax-free was shown in the bravado of spirit merchants in London, who for many years, openly advertised the gin as 'Genuine Crow Link'. (endnote: H.M.Coastguards Emperor Napoleon Bonaparte Scarlettwww.hansonclan.co.uk/napoleon.htm)

Small efforts had been made to try and recoup taxes on goods arriving on the shores of Britain. In 1698, the Treasury and Board of Customs set up a team of around 300 men as 'Riding Officers' in Kent and Sussex to patrol the coastline. By 1809 they were backed up by the 'Preventative Waterguard' who were allocated Watch Houses on the cliff's edge; their sole duty to patrol the coast in small boats through the night. Smugglers, however, after centuries of cunning were still able to break through these defensive measures, even after the establishment of the Coastguard service on 15th January 1822, which swelled its force to 6,700 men.

Smugglers off Beachy Head. © R. Wassell

For the smugglers, Birling Gap, just west of the lighthouse, was the perfect cove to land their ill-gotten gains. Long before the fashion for sea-bathing, the beaches were isolated, surrounded only by small hamlets high up on the cliffs. To land their goods the smugglers disguised their boats by painting them black and raising dark sails, making them all but invisible from the shore. They kept a vigilant watch of the patrolling customs man or riding officer. The smugglers would use various lights to signal to the collaborating 'spotsman' on the beach that they were approaching with another hoard. His job was to signal back that the coast was clear, literally, letting them know that everything was in place to move the goods quickly inland. At the time, crude methods were used by the 'spotsman' such as waving a lantern into the night but harsher penalties were imposed for those signalling to ships at sea, as they were often the cause of shipwrecks. Thus the spotsman had to find more sophisticated and wily methods to signal to the smugglers. Instead, they would place the lantern in a cave such as Parson Darby's hole, which meant the light could only be seen by the smugglers at sea, but not by those patrolling the land.

Later, houses were built with small windows in the roof where a lantern could innocently signal out to sea: 'Technology came to the rescue, too, in the form of the spout lantern. As the name suggests, this had a long spout in front of the flame, sometimes with a bulls-eye of glass to focus the beam. An even more distinctive lantern used a primitive rotating shutter to produce a regularly flashing light.' (endnote: History of Smuggling. Signalling and communications. www.smuggling.co.uk/gazetteer_se_16.html)

Once the goods reached the shore the next task was arranged by a 'lander' to haul them up the vertical cliffs. This was done by gathering gang members on the beach as tub carriers. The contraband was loaded onto pallets, usually old farm gates, or piled into baskets and tubs and hoisted on a wheeled derrick from a horse-driven winch on the headland, up the face of the cliffs. When the smugglers were unable to use a derrick they simply threw the cases of tea or spirits over their shoulders and carried the haul up dangerous, swaying rope ladders. Many, unsurprisingly, did not make it to the top and perished at the foot of the cliffs.

In July 1828 the smugglers tried to haul 37 tubs of spirits to the top of the cliffs but were interrupted by the firing of blockade sentries and had to drop 12 barrels back to the shore to make good their escape. The goods that made it to the headland were then loaded onto pack horses and driven to London or hidden at the gangs' headquarters in local inns. These small guesthouses indicated their co-operation with the smugglers by planting rows of lime trees outside their doors.

The smugglers have received little credit for their expert seamanship. Where many professional sailors floundered on the low-lying sands the smugglers were able to navigate close to the shoreline, usually in the darkness of night. Local knowledge of the shifting tides aided their bountiful landings. However, they were often known to bribe local fishermen to bring them across the Channel or engage the services of French vessels.

Whether wrecked by the unforgiving coastline, drunken captains or malicious greed many lives have been lost on this small stretch of Sussex land, their souls forever caught in the wind.

Smugglers

Chapter 10

A Smuggler's Tale

The romantic image of the smugglers, made famous in literature and movies, rarely tells the true story of the violent, ruthless methods they used in order to avoid capture. One such gang was led by Stanton Collins, working from Market Cross House (now called Ye Olde Smugglers Inn) in the nearby village of Alfriston. The Inn itself was the perfect hiding place with 21 rooms, 6 staircases, 48 doors and a tunnel network leading to outside buildings. From here, they planned their illicit trade safe from the authorities. Although they did have a reputation for being particularly adept at avoiding coastguards they were largely helped by the local villagers who were often only too pleased to buy their goods. But one event has survived into folklore which involved the brutal murder of a patrolling customs man: 'Fearing that his attentions would interfere with their landing, the gang moved the lumps of white chalk that the officer used as way-markers for his moonlight sorties along the cliff-edge. Instead of leading him safely along the coast path, the stones lured the poor man over the parapet. Hearing his cries as he tumbled from the precipice, the gang emerged from hiding, only to find the man desperately hanging by his fingertips. Deaf to his pleas for mercy, one of the gang cynically trod on their adversary's fingertips, sending him tumbling on the rocks below.' (endnote: Smugglers Britain. www.smuggling.co.uk/gazetteer_se_16.html.

The brave coastguards were often faced with perilous danger, and not just because of the violent smugglers. When a boat was spotted they would have to navigate their way down the cliffs to the shore to apprehend the outlaws, seizing the goods, retrieving it all back up to the top. Most of them were not local to the area as the Admiralty was afraid that too much proximity to the smugglers would result in corruption or collaboration with them.

In the 1820s, the East Sussex Preventative Waterguards were housed in no less than four Watch Houses along the Seven Sisters cliffs spread out over four miles, covering: Beachy Head, Birling Gap, Crowlink and Cuckmere. Birling Gap (Birling meaning Gaelic for boat) has access to the shore even to this day but only via wooden steps which are removed when the weather becomes unpredictable and stormy. In the 19th century, Crowlink was also accessible from the shore by way of a small slipway but this, and the path to

Birling Gap beach. © R. Wassell

one of the coastguard's cottages, have been reclaimed by the sea through constant cliff erosion.

The Preventatives kept in touch with one another by a path on the cliff edge which they marked with small heaps of fresh chalk that was so white it was even visible on the darkest of nights. It was the only safe way to walk the headland without accidentally walking straight over the sheer drop.

In the 1820s three men and their families shared the hazardous job at Crowlink. The dwellings consisted of one block of whitewashed buildings, divided into two separate living spaces and a cottage, now in ruins, hanging over the cliff. Mark Johnstone, a stern man in his 50s, lived in one of these buildings with his 13-year-old son, Ted, a devoted child who was harshly treated by his old seadog of a father, a sea veteran who had served under Nelson on the Nile.

The second Preventative was the youthful looking, John Hardwick, aged 43 who had a matching, young-at-heart personality. He lived with his wife and seven-year-old daughter, Mary.

The third, Gordon McNaish, at 32 was already widowed. Although he had a cottage of his own the quiet Scotsman moved into a room with the Hardwicks after his wife passed away. As he had no children of his own he doted on little Mary. He was only ever known to rally his Celtic temper, which spilled into foul language even around the pious Mrs Hardwick, whenever he saw young Ted being cruelly beaten by Johnstone.

Still, Ted would go wherever his father did which included, by day, summer excursions onto the beach, collecting fresh lobsters and shellfish. As his father fished, Ted indulged in childish activities, splashing about in the waves, soaking up the sunrays in shallow rock pools or climbing the boulders looking for adventure. As well as practising his swimming in the cold channel building his strength, as he was promised to the King to pursue his duty as a sailor by Johnstone, who, having served on a ship that sunk during a brutal navy battle, was obsessed with his son being able to survive. Other times, even on cold winter days, Ted was treated as any grown man carrying a burden of driftwood from nearby Cuckmere Haven, his small body bent under the weight.

One particular quiet, sunny, January day, Ted and his father were collecting wood. After a few hours, they stopped for a rest. A low sea fog high on the cliffs had hampered their journey home and was beginning to thicken, as sunset came in. Ted, unloading his sticks went, as usual, to peer over the edge out to sea. He suddenly let out a yelp and ran back to where his father was resting. He shouted: 'A boat, dad!' His father sternly replied: 'Curse ye! Ye young fool. Did they see we?' Without an answer, Johnstone strode to the edge, threw himself down onto his belly and crawled his way to the brink.

Below him, he saw a small boat rowing towards the shore slowly and cautiously on the high tide; five men sat in the boat, with a bulky load stowed under tarpaulin. Amongst them was a familiar figure in a wide three-cornered hat, his face turned upwards, revealing a large patch over one eye.

'Blinker!' Johnstone called back to his son. 'And they're making for the Haven!' Jumping to his feet, Johnstone grabbed his son's shoulder and pointed. Then Ted shouted: 'There's a ship!'

Out on the horizon just a mile and a half away, Johnstone could just make out the silhouette of a hull. 'French,' he muttered under his breath: 'I could tell her cut anywhere.' Using the fog for cover, the French ship had crept close to the shore and unloaded the contraband onto Blinker Eldridge's boat for landing. 'Blinker' was well known to the coastguards having escaped capture on many occasions; he was also known as 'the prince of contraband'. The closest the coastguards had come to capturing him was during a scuffle where a pistol shot had been fired into the dark, close enough to take out Eldridge's left eye. He made his escape but since that day he had worn a heavy leather patch, much like the racehorses wore, giving him the notorious name of 'Blinker'.

Johnstone was excited at the thought of catching such a famous outlaw. Calling back to Ted he formed a plan so clever that a general would have been proud. He told the boy to run home and alert the other Preventatives and get them to launch a boat to come around the cliff end. His intention was to hold the smugglers up until they arrived. Dusk was now upon them with the watch tower invisible in the twilight fog. Johnstone could tell from the high tide that the smugglers would be afraid of being spotted by the coastguards at Cuckmere Haven (the cottages featured in the film *Atonement* based on a book by Ian McEwan) so would probably hug the eastern shore to avoid detection. He would have to find an observation point quickly. Johnstone hid behind an ant hill slightly inland just far enough away from the sheer drop where the land graduated less steeply. Darkness added to his cover as he lay face down; then he took out his two pistols and laid them on a mound directly in front of him.

As the cold, damp, January chills crept into his bones he could barely hear any noise from the shore below above his own shivering, until suddenly he heard the distinct 'plop' of oars hitting the sea. Squinting his eyes he was able to make out a deeper shadow on the water 30 to 40 yards out. Fearing the smugglers would escape he took up one of the pistols, firing blindly into the night. A shout rang out followed by two retaliating gunshots which flew inches wide of where he lay. Just then rapid footsteps came upon him and a small body fell to his side. It was Ted. Johnstone was angry with his son for risking his life by coming back, but Ted stayed where he was and calmly took the pistol and began to reload it for his father. They stopped again to listen.

Way below, they heard the sound of the smugglers cautiously wading onto the shallow shore. The boat had stopped seemingly about to turn back out to sea. Johnstone had to act. Raising his pistol he fired again. The flash from the gunpowder for a moment lit the scene: the boat was hugging the bank, a direct hit lilting it slightly where water was seeping into the hull.

Some of the smugglers started to climb up the hillside no doubt to ambush their attackers. Ted grew scared and asked his father what they should do if the smugglers surrounded them, but before his father could answer, a shot was fired from the boat, hitting the ant hill, showering mud and grass into Johnstone's face. Blindly, he shot back as another blast came back at him, this time wounding him in his right hand. 'Curse 'em! They've got me!' he cried

Chapter 11

Myths, ghosts and legends

Is it haunted or cursed this lonely corner of outstanding beauty? Some say that ghosts use evil forces to lure the weak and vulnerable to jump. There are many tales of 'a horrifying monk in black' who entices people to their deaths; he is said to have fled from Henry VIII's soldiers during the ethnic cleansing of his kingdom when the king ordered all monasteries, convents, cathedrals, and churches to be shut down and the abbots and monks to be instantly slaughtered. The monk ran for his life, avoiding capture before finally finding refuge in a stately home set deep in the South Downs.

For a while the monk was safe, helping out with daily chores in return for his keep, until one fateful day. The Lord of the manor came upon him quietly praying and callously betrayed him to the Crown. Soldiers arrested him, dragging him from his sanctuary, shackled in chains. He was then taken to Beachy Head and thrown, mercilessly, from the cliff top. As he was being dragged to his death he was heard calling out a chilling curse. Two weeks later the Lord's estate mysteriously burned to the ground.

The monk has been spotted on the cliffs many times, still dressed in his clerical robes, pointing a finger towards the fatal edge.

Smugglers were known to create elaborate tales, scaring the locals enough to stay home while they carried out their bountiful toil. Yet there is no denying that there is something extraordinary on this windswept headland that profoundly affects people, and with so many tragic and wretched souls trapped in the aura, it's hard to ignore. As Louis de Bernieres wrote:

'I had to leave Beachy Head. Every human being has known times of the most abject and implacable despair, and it was impossible not to feel profoundly what was in the hearts of those sorrowing souls. Knowing and imagining, I found it hard to keep back the tears even though the place is lovely. Either their infinite pain is imprinted upon the atmosphere or one has the illusion that it is. All about are the wisps and traces of broken hearts, cancelled dreams, abandoned expectations. Here are the ghosts of those who loved others too much or themselves too little, of those lost battles with insanity, of those driven to heartsickness by an oppressive sense of futility and the apparent absence of

God, of those who defiantly and courageously denied a terminal illness its tortures. Here also are the sad small ghosts of those whose existence nobody noticed until they became a mess to clear away.' (*Harpers* 1996)

The words he wrote so eloquently are felt by many who, on arriving at this divine cosmos, quail, or are forever enchanted.

One dusky evening in 1976 a man was walking his dog across the Downs as usual when he suddenly noticed the figure of a young woman who seemed to be dressed in an old-fashioned long grey dress, coming towards him. His dog spotted her too; huddling against his owner, he began a low growling, his shaggy coat bristling with fear. As the man stood watching, the ghostly figure drew closer and bent down to stroke the dog which let out a fierce howl, as if he had been viciously beaten, and ran away. At that very moment the figure disappeared. The man finally found his terrified dog cowering in the gorse bushes and headed back to town to recount his story to all who would listen.

He was assured that 'the lady in grey' was often seen on the cliff path by locals. They believe that she is a phantom of a suicide that occurred in the 1850s. Three more sightings of her were reported in the latter half of 1978.

Another ghost spoken of is 'a farmer's wife' who carries a bundle that appears to be a small child. She is seen hugging it close to her breast before taking two fateful steps straight over the edge. Legend has it that she is the widow of a farmer brutally murdered in Victorian times. She too has been recently spotted but only ever in the evening.

Further West along the coast at Seaford, a road cuts through the chalk inland towards the village of Alfriston called the White Way. At the crossroads a white dog used to appear on Midsummer's Eve, only every seven years. It is thought he was owned by the Chowne estate in the 18th century; he served two masters who, on a stroll back to their home one evening, were murdered by robbers and then callously buried in a shallow grave at a crossroads. Sometimes the dog was sighted with one of these masters, and it was considered very bad luck to cross their spectral paths, as it usually ended in accident or death. A song has survived, reminding locals to be wary:

When evening closes in with shadows grey,
and ghostly vapours overhang White Way,
and the crescent moon hangs gloomy in the west,
'tis then the spirit of young Chowne can't rest
but walks abroad with melancholy stride,
adown the path that skirts the chalk hill-side

The legend began exactly seven years after the two men had met their fate, when a country girl and her lover, on a stroll on the hillside, saw the ghosts, and were so terrified, they ran for their lives. Another seven years passed. On this night several men were drinking at a local Inn discussing the ghosts. One man expressed his disbelief in the existence of ghosts and, bravely, no doubt through the charms of alcohol, decided to walk the White Way home. As he reached the crossroads, the dog appeared, following him along the path before disappearing down an embankment. Two days later the same man suffered a terrible fall, breaking his leg. These events continued into the 19th century until a road-widening scheme uncovered the remains of the two murdered men; their bones were finally given a Christian burial. The dog has never appeared since.

All the phantom sightings are associated with violent deaths. Perhaps the ghosts of human sacrifice also walk these cliffs of despair. In 1995 the Archaeology correspondent, David Keys, for the *Independent* newspaper reported evidence of 'Probable prehistoric human sacrifice.' On a dig, at a site close to Eastbourne, archaeologists from University College London made an amazing discovery of a Bronze Age temple. They found 'part of a skeleton of a child aged around five, an adult leg bone, part of a human skull and a human tooth at a 2,600-2,800-year-old ritual complex located in what used to be an arc of marshland between the South Downs and the Channel. The human remains were unearthed together with the deliberately smashed remnants of butchered cattle, pigs and sheep. Amber beads, part of a bridle, and bronze tools, several of which had also been deliberately broken, were found. All the items appear to have been dropped or thrown into the marsh from a platform linked to the land by a wooden causeway.'(endnote: © Newspaper Publishing PLC. ProQuest Information and Learning Company. Human sacrifice site unearthed.
http://findarticles.com/p/articles/mi_qn4158/archives).

Maybe that's why witches' covens have long existed on the South Downs too. The custom, in olden times, of witches impersonating the ritual of the Wild Hunt still haunts Sussex. Doreen Valiente, a practising witch in East Sussex until her death in 1999, records in her book *Witchcraft for Tomorrow* that witches were said to reenact 'a cavalcade of wildly galloping riders, dressed in the costumes of an earlier age, and headed by some mythical figure or ancient hero.'

Today, when the headland takes on its sinister, misty solitude, the spirit of this old practice takes on 'an eerie visitation, as on Ditchling Beacon, the highest point of the South Downs, when on winter nights, as old Sussex people will tell, the sound of the Wild Hunt, with its galloping horses, baying hounds and yelling hunters, approaches and rushes by, though nothing at all can be seen.'

Proof of witches has been found in artefacts uncovered on Beachy Head.

Valiente goes on to write: 'A witch sign that was used in olden times in the county of Sussex, and perhaps elsewhere, was the number thirteen written in Roman numerals, thus XIII. Among the Sussex witchcraft objects in my collection are an old pewter candlestick with the 'XIII' marking on it, and two very old spoons, probably once used to stir some witch's brew, that bare the same marking.' (endnote: Valiente Doreen (1987) *Witchcraft for Tomorrow* Robert Hale Ltd London. First published 1978).

Bus stop at the top of Beachy Head. © K. J. Varney

Doreen Valiente has written about many rituals in Sussex, believing in the 1950s that East Sussex heralded a revival in witchcraft where covens worshipped an unidentified earth mother and sky father, performing rites with modern magical tools, while consulting the *Book of Shadows.*

The number 13 that Valiente writes about is still an obscure presence on the Downs. The council-run bus service to the very top of Beachy Head is curiously numbered 12A, and 13 on Sundays, which both relate to witchcraft and superstition. In particular, the number 13 is associated with bad luck and magical power that is still openly shunned in today's society, because it is central to ancient traditions of sacred geometry, reflected in a pattern existing in man, nature and the heavens:

- In Scotland there is no terminal 13 (or 12A) in any airport, 12B is used instead.
- According to Wicca there is a maximum of 13 witches in a coven.
- The 13th Tarot card is represented as Death.
- In Egyptian lore there are 13 steps between life and death.
- History records that there were 13 steps up to the gallows.
- The 13th rune represents a point between light and dark (heaven and the underworld).
- There are 13 major joints in the body.
- There are 13 lunar cycles in a solar year.

- The moon travels 13 degrees across the sky every day.
- Of 15 UK National Parks the South Downs is number 13

'The Aztec calendar once said that "thirteen is the basic structural unit in nature. It means the attracting centre around which elements focus and collect." Is this, then, the reason for Christ's 12 disciples, King Arthur's 12 nights or the 12 major constellations in relation to our sun?'

Harry Ward served 13 years at Beachy Head, there are 13 cameras focused on the Golden Gate Bridge looking for would be jumpers! (endnote: www.thevesselofgod.com/thirteen.html

As you watch the bus snake up the cliff road it is hard not to wonder whether stepping onto the number 13, for anyone considering ending their life when they alight, is seen as a sign or confirmation that they are indeed doomed.

Society often has a vivid imagination when it comes to supernatural possession; the teachings of early Christian thinkers have never quite left the realms of consciousness. The pagans who refused to embrace Christianity after the 7th century had many tales of the Devil's work right across the South Downs. St Dunstan, a devout monk, was known for his legendary cunning at defeating the Devil. He encountered the Devil on the Downs around 900AD when the Devil told him he was going to knock down all the houses in the local village. St Dunstan made a pact with the Devil to leave standing any house with a horseshoe hanging outside. The Devil agreed. St Dunstan rushed to the village, calling at every cottage, urging the villagers to nail horseshoes swiftly above their doors, and the whole village was saved.

The Devil had no intention of letting St Dunstan beat him and resorted to cunning tactics to try and catch him out. One day as the monk was busy working in the local forge with the blacksmith, the Devil appeared in the doorway. He was disguised as a beautiful woman and began distracting him with talk of spiritual matters. Soon 'the woman' began flirting, but St Dunstan spotted a cloven hoof under the girl's dress. He picked up his red-hot tongs, clamping them to the Devil's nose. The Devil, shrieking with pain, fled to Tunbridge Wells in Kent and plunged into the water. As legend has it; this is why the water is so iron-rich and notably warmer.

The Devil is also known for his particular loathing of farmers' wives. This is thought to be because of an incident where he was caught out by a clever farmer's wife. Apparently, he was so enraged at the amount of churches being built that he set about digging a huge channel through the South Downs; the idea was to allow the sea water to escape onto the land which would drown its growing population. One night an old farmer's wife saw what he was up to, so she crept out into the darkness, lit a candle behind her cooking sieve, and knocked her sleeping cockerel from his perch with a hurl of a stone. The Devil, hearing the cock crow and mistaking the flickering light for an early sunrise fled with the job only half-finished. Once again, the Devil had been defeated. To this day, the Channel is known as Devil's Dyke.

A pinnacle to the east of the lighthouse is named Devil's Chimney. The Victorian occultist and mountaineer, Aleister Crowley, either cursed or predicted that if it ever fell, Eastbourne would perish. Crowley often attempted a climb up the crumbling 'chimney' with his friend and student, Francis Israel Regardie, a member of the Golden Dawn, (a magical order of spiritual development).

Crowley recorded that he had left his mother reading a book at a scenic spot further along the cliffs while he, once again, climbed the Devil's Chimney. He heard a cry, considered impossible from such a distance. When he rushed back to where he had left his mother hours before, he found she had slipped down the cliff face, and was in urgent need of rescuing, almost becoming another statistic.

Crowley widely wrote about his hedonistic experiences as a sanctuary for the traveller on the path of enlightenment. The Esoteric Order of the Golden Dawn, founded in 1888, was an extension of the ancient Mysteries of the Light, offering initiation into the hidden knowledge of the mysticism of life. Believing he held the secrets of a pathway to the spiritual light, his work became erratic, even dangerous. Regardie, like many others in the group, including poet W. B. Yeats, soon tired of Crowley's practice and manifestations. He had become an uncontrollable astral junkie, too unstable to maintain, and their friendship soon ended. Breaking away from the earlier teachings, Crowley began to publish the magical secrets of the Knowledge Lectures of the Outer Order which cast the Golden Dawn into a dormant cycle. With the secrets revealed there seemed little point in carrying on. All the Temple banners along with personal magical instruments were buried in a cliff top garden at Beachy Head.

Thirty years later in the autumn of 1966, the cliffs crumbled away and a box of these magical artefacts fell into the sea. The box was discovered by tourists who had been strolling along the beach. Once again the secrets of the Golden Dawn were exposed. *The Daily Telegraph* newspaper published photos of them along with a statement, claiming they belonged to a witch.

In 2001, the Devil's Chimney was unexpectedly sent crashing into the sea, creating a 70m long spit between the shore and the lighthouse. News of this sent shock waves of fear through those who knew about Crowley's sinister prediction. Although neither death nor damage resulted in the collapse, a coven of local witches, fearing that Crowley's curse would come true, descended on Beachy Head that June to ritually cleanse the aura. For days they stayed on the headland, chanting and casting white spells until they were satisfied that the curse had been reversed. Their presence proved that whether the stories are magic or myth much of society still believes in the Devil and his association with tempting the vulnerable and the depressed. Professor Mark Williams describes in his study *Suicide and Attempted Suicide:* 'It can feel as though they have been taken over by something outside themselves. The Devil metaphor matches and gives shape to this inner feeling, even for those who would normally reject supernatural explanations of experience.' (endnote: (1997)Williams Mark *Suicide and Attempted Suicide* Penguin Books London)

Despite his failures over the centuries the Devil does seem to have kept a prominent place in the history of East Sussex, if he has any influence on the suicidal mind that has to be considered carefully by mental health practitioners, councillors and psychoanalysts. But his presence in the South Downs cannot be denied. His reputation as a tempter who could urge victims to commit suicide must surely be examined. Many have endeavoured to rid the cliffs of his influence. Exorcisms have periodically been conducted on the headland. Keith Lane experienced this with a local spiritualist just a few years ago. In an attempt to find some peace at one particular spot, she recited white incantations at the place where two young people had recently leapt to their deaths, close to where his wife had taken her own life. She believed that the spirit of a known paedophile who had jumped from the cliffs was now luring young people to jump from the same spot. As she scattered cleansing salt during chanting, Keith stood closely by, laying flowers in memory of his wife's birthday.

It was a still day, the easterly breeze unusually quiet. As Keith stepped back from the edge he recalls, vividly, how, as he placed the flowers on the ground, a 'short, gusty, really chilly wind' lifted the flowers into the air, pinning them to the face of the cliff. As he stood watching, the whole bouquet rose up high in the air, like it was dancing in the wind. As it came back down, each petal was plucked from its stem, floating delicately, and settling down to rest by Maggie's wooden cross. A peace descended.

Cliffs and high places are thought to be spiritually protected by the Archangel Raphael. He is the first of four Great Archangels and Master of the Powers of Light. If you stand on the cliffs and look directly east into a dawning spring day it is said that his radiant image will appear; his hair billowing like sunbeams as he stands before you cool and erect. Embroidered on his chest is the image of Aquarius, indicating insight and truth, everlasting life and the eternal belief in all humanity. In his hand he carries an upright sword of Damocles, reflecting fragments of diamond light flashes into the rising sun. Raphael's power is to touch the mind and thoughts of the faithless. His sword represents peace, and is raised in protection of our mental will, cutting away the burdens of our troubled minds. As you watch this wonder from the edge of the world you will see him raising his sword as a salute, silently turning his face out across the mists of sunrise on the horizon then lowering his sword to his feet with the glittering hilt uppermost, and spreading his wings in passive protection.

'The sword of Raphael is the Sword of Peace, and lies at the end of the Rainbow Bridge of Faith between God and Man.' (endnote: Order of the White Lion ©J.Shell 1981-2006)

By his side you may also catch a glimpse of a misty, shadowy shape, opaque in the hazy blue sky, darting through the clouds on the edge of the wind. He is Paralda, Lord of the Element of Air, who is charged with controlling the movement of air and thought patterns around the earth. He swoops freely across the skies with delicate wings; his hair glimmers from the sunlight as he melts into the grey whiteness of the clouds; his eyes, ever darting and alert, are silver-slanted moonbeams that come to rest on you as gently as the spring breeze. Yet, in just one glance, he can capture the darkest secrets of your innermost thoughts, becoming suddenly as wild and unpredictable as the easterly wind, his voice a rushing sound merging with the squall. It is with these breathy sounds he evokes the arrival of tiny, elf-like elemental beings called Sylphs. Watch closely and you will see them as they flock around him a waiflike blur of eerie sapphire and grey. All these spiritual guides are there as elemental, surreal entities to entrance the troubled soul, heal the broken-hearted or guide you to the other kingdom. (endnote: Order of the White Lion. www.orderofthewhitelion.com/theelements@Elementals/Paralda.htm)

Devil, ghost, sacrifice or spectre, this lonely place has a unique magnetism that draws deep into the turbulent soul. Whatever lures the hopeless here is as certain as the stars returning to shine long after their light has flickered into darkness. Every spiritual nature has visited, created an aura then left without it. On the duskiest night the beam from the lighthouse seems to catch swirls chasing each other before dropping into the ripples below, the platinum reflection mirrored by the moon. Shadows on the headland no longer moving, just one dark space.

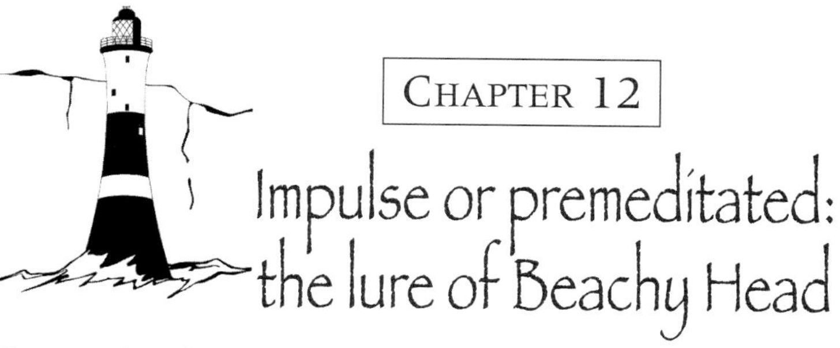

CHAPTER 12

Impulse or premeditated: the lure of Beachy Head

Overcoming the spectacle of nature, the cliffs tempt and taunt you to defy it, and take a chance. Grooming you to trust the safety of the edge, to sit or lie on the brink of the ends of the earth, on God's lap. Even the most fearful will have a single moment of unease, wondering what it might be like to fall. The bright white cliffs like the bright white light of the infinite.

Most of the suicides and many attempted suicides occur directly above or around the two lighthouse buildings at Beachy Head. Many more happen just east and west of the newer lighthouse where the terrain is steep and craggy. There are recorded stories of people surviving a fall here, by landing on the dangerous narrow ledges.

Beachy Head. © K. J. Varney

In September 2004 a woman drove her 4x4 Mitsubishi Shogun car, at speed, towards the cliff edge. Lifeboat crews were later told by witnesses that just before she went over they saw her brake lights flash on, perhaps changing her mind at the last minute. One witness reported: 'I was looking down to the lighthouse when I saw this 4x4 go past me to the right. I thought something was wrong because I've never seen anyone drive a vehicle so close to the edge. Then just before it disappeared from my sight I saw the brake lights go on. There was nothing anyone could do.' (endnote: Lucky to be alive. A woman cheated death after driving off Beachy Head in a car *Eastbourne Herald* published 29/09/04)

Frantic 999 calls were made and at 1.30pm coastguards at Dover received a call from Sussex Ambulance Control with a report that the car had gone over east of the lighthouse. When the rescue teams arrived they could see the vehicle wedged sideways in an unstable position 90 ft from the cliff top. The police helicopter, 'Hotel 900', circled the area and from their vantage seaward viewpoint, sent back the message that the woman had managed to crawl out of the car by the passenger side window and was now lying in front of the vehicle.

The first objective for her rescuers was to secure the car; any wrong move would endanger their lives and the safe rescue of the patient. At this point they had no idea of the extent of her injuries. The Fire and Rescue Service began by securing a cable into the cliff top and lowering a specially trained coastguard over the cliff to counterbalance the car by tying the other end to the lurching bumper. With the car safely secured, the coastguard then quickly assessed the distressed patient who, amazingly, was not only fully conscious but was found to have suffered only minor cuts and bruises. Dangling on the rock face her rescuer continued to reassure her until another coastguard was lowered over the edge to assist her safe removal from under the vehicle. (endnote: *Eastbourne Herald.* Driver rescued from cliff gully. First published September 28th 2004)

This dramatic rescue, unusually, has a happy ending. Only 5% of jumpers survive, largely depending on where, along the four miles, they jump or drive off.

However, access on to the Downs, even in a four-wheel drive cross-country vehicle, is challenging. The kerb has been double-banked to try to prevent cars approaching either accidentally or intentionally. Behind this safety barrier is a harsh, natural incline from the road meaning that only those with an absolute fortitude are able to thrust the vehicle over the grassy verge, through 100m of rough terrain, maintaining an acceleration that will propel the car over the edge.

It is a decision that can be averted at any time but still it appears that once the decision has been made neither God nor man can stop them.

On Friday, 31st August 2007, 25-year-old student, Hinah Shah, drove her blue Ford escort from her home in Hove, Brighton to the cliffs of Beachy Head. At 10.30pm, she plunged into the sea.

Wreck at the base of the cliffs. © R. Wassell

When the coastguards arrived they saw the car crushed on the cliff face, and just about made out Hinah's body which had been thrown from the vehicle and was lying on the jagged rocks below at Peacehaven. The treacherous, stormy weather made it impossible for the cliff rescue team to recover her remains. So her body remained there all night. It wasn't until 1.30pm the next day that the team began their rescue; as the weather was still bad, it took them three and a half hours to recover her body.

While some arrive at the cliff top and hurl themselves off almost immediately, many others have been known to visit the cliffs time and again before finally taking their own lives.

This was almost the case for local man, Jon Curtis. While on a visit to New York he took an overdose of tablets while high on cocaine. After 10 days in intensive care he came home to England, and found a job at a manufacturing company. But the suicidal thoughts hadn't left him. One day he was feeling really down having spent all his month's wages in one weekend on drugs: 'I chose Beachy Head because I knew that if I went over it would be final. I ended up pretending in my head that I didn't have to be in work until later then drove to the Belle Tout lighthouse.'

Parking his car in the empty car park he remembers clearly thinking that there was no need to buy a parking ticket, yet he strangely locked his car and headed towards the cliffs. 'I didn't have any real clear thoughts except that, but my boss had been worried after I hadn't turned up, so he called my closest friend.' Jon didn't answer her calls.

It was only when the name of his boss began flashing on his mobile screen that he felt able to answer. 'When I told him what I was doing he snapped me out of it by calling me a prat and to think of how my parents would feel having to deal with it.'

After the call, Jon remembered that his boss had lost a brother in America in a drive-by shooting and felt that his message was heartfelt. So he left the cliffs that day and life seemed to settle for a while but in August 2006, wracked with despair, Jon once again found himself returning to the cliffs. For six days he lived in his car near a tiny hamlet called Crowlink, just a mile west of the lighthouse, fighting a battle with his conscience, guilty about those he'd leave behind against his own desperate hopelessness.

Using the local leisure centre he would shower, wandering amongst others unseen before returning to his car with foil-warm food of assorted takeaways, moving his car now and again to different viewpoints. He never spoke to anyone, just sat watching, hour after hour in the front seat of his car, watching the constant patrols of the chaplains from the Beachy Head Chaplaincy Team. No one saw him.

On the sixth day he wrote a final farewell. 'I don't know why I didn't write a note the first time. I have tried to remember but never can. It was hard to write the note as it seems very final doing that and you imagine what people are going to think when reading it as sometimes I came across very blunt so when writing the note I didn't want people thinking it was just some matter of fact thing I was doing. It definitely made me think of the no going back once I jumped. It did take quite a while to write the note but it seems hard to remember what I put. Most of it was saying sorry for doing it and what songs I wanted at my funeral.' Once he had written the note, he placed it on the passenger seat then drove his car back to the same car park opposite the decommissioned Belle Tout Lighthouse.

The cliffs at this summit are 325 ft above the sea but are nevertheless as sheer and lethal as the higher points. He describes this desperate episode in chilling detail. 'I edged towards the cliff edge and peered over whilst on my stomach. I dropped some rocks off and counted how long they took to fall, and thought that I would definitely die if I jumped. It was quite a sunny day and there were some foreign students near me chatting. As I was sitting down I felt very tired from all the strain of what to do and fell asleep. I woke up a few hours later, my head had cleared for some reason so I went to my car and drove home.'

Asking Jon questions was very difficult and his written responses were punctuated by long breaks, indicating the fear of his previous intentions. Although he is reassuring with his replies, when they come, there is still a shadow of anguish: 'I definitely think it's behind me now as I don't feel drawn to it like I was before.'

With the fatality of the act of self-sacrifice at these cliffs few people can give a true and honest insight into the biggest quandary of all, why? Jon replies: 'I think the main lure of Beachy Head is there is no survival if you jump properly, whereas if you take tablets you can throw up or go to Accident & Emergency; the lighthouse is like a target of some sort, what with the red and white stripes like a bullseye.'

Car smashed in the gorse at Beachy Head. © K. J. Varney

And finally, considering that most suicides at Beachy Head take place at the bright dawn of day contrary to the belief that most suicides are committed in the dark of night, Jon offers a unique peek into the minds of the disillusioned: 'The fact it was sunny didn't really deter me from doing it but I think to some people a bright day may well make them think that once they jump all the darkness in their heads will be gone and that's what it's like for them.'

The reality of the lethal act hit home in September 2007 when Jon was walking with his girlfriend the length of the Downs. As they strolled along they suddenly heard the rotors of the coastguard helicopter 'India Juliet'. Moments later the couple saw the cliff rescue team winching a body up the cliffs while paramedics waited on the cliff top, ready to check for signs of life. The body was later identified as 45-year-old Melanie Wells, wife of former Sussex and England cricketer, Alan Wells. On a bright Saturday morning, overcome with depression, she carefully placed her handbag on the grassy ledge near the old lighthouse then began a slow walk along the cliff, before taking the final step over the edge, she had previously visited the cliffs on May 15th after taking an overdose but later returned home. She left behind her devastated husband and two small sons.

At that moment, Jon suddenly felt an overwhelming empathy with the emergency services: 'I had a gruesome view of what happens when you do jump; it's a horrid job for them to do.'

This incident changed Jon's mind for good about his own suicidal intentions. He is now a 'born-again Christian' and has a renewed focus on life, and has even revisited New York. No one approached him on the cliff edge in his moments of despair, and sometimes this hypnotic place can appear isolated. Yet the Beachy Head Chaplaincy Team, who patrol the cliffs to try and talk down any would-be jumpers, intervened on an incredible 670 incidents in 2007, of which 248 people were found to be depressed or suicidal: 27 others were tragically missed. In 2008 there were 699 incidents of which 217 were suicidal, 27 perished.

One jumper who was missed by the team in 2007 was Michael Payne, a 65-year-old, retired telecommunications engineer. He and his wife had left their Hailsham home on a sunny Monday morning on the 18th June 2007 for a drive to Beachy Head. Parking the car at Birling Gap they got out and went for a stroll. As they hiked across the Downs his wife Janet tripped on a rabbit hole, hurting her ankle. After helping her back to the car he was suddenly struck with an anxiety attack, asking her over and over how he would manage if anything happened to her. He had been sinking into a depression for the past year after experiencing a prickling sensation in his arm.

Wracked with panic he got out of the car, ignoring his wife's pleas. Once he was out of her sight, he ran past onlookers, dodging the Beachy Head Chaplain, Ross Hardy, who had seen him walking to the edge several times before. However, Ross could only watch as Michael started to run towards the edge of the cliffs; he jumped off before anyone could stop him.

His wife had no idea what had happened so sat waiting in the car unsure what to do and full of dread. After an hour she painfully limped, checking the cliff top before deciding to drive back down the hill to look for him. As she turned the car into the bottom of the incline, she was dazzled by flashing blue lights and high visibility yellow and silver striped police jackets. Her life had changed forever.

Michael Payne's demise almost seems like an impulsive act, but many suicides on Beachy Head are premeditated. On Monday 4th of January 2005, Exeter police were alerted to a couple missing from their caravan home in Tedburn St Mary, Devon since Sunday night. The information was passed on to Sussex police who raised the alarm with the Dover Coastguard. Immediately, the Eastbourne cliff rescue team, police, lifeboats and paramedics began searching the cliffs at Beachy Head.

At 9.10 that morning, they reported the discovery of two bodies: a man in his 50s and a woman of around 60. They were lying on protruding flint and chalk rocks 50 yards apart, 150 ft above the beach, and 400 ft below the headland.

A note was found which simply said: 'Do not resuscitate.'

At their inquest the following August the coroner, Mr Alan Craze, was given the harrowing details that led to their deaths. Terry Heley, 51, and his wife Olive, 65, had been arrested the previous November. Mrs Heley had been released without charge but Mr Heley had been bailed to appear at Portsmouth

Crown Court, facing charges of one rape, and 22 separate charges of gross indecency against three children from 30 years ago.

While awaiting trial it appears the couple went to Beachy Head, had a last couple of drinks in the hilltop pub, then stepped off the edge of the world together. Their only daughter told the coroner's court: 'They couldn't bear the possibility of being separated, even though they knew they were innocent. I'm sure they decided quite rationally to take their lives to ensure they would be together for ever.' Mr Alan Craze called it 'a classic suicide pact.' Details have never been released as to whether Terry Heley would have been found guilty of the alleged crimes. (endnote: Rape suspect and wife in suicide pact. *The Guardian* pub: Aug 24 2005)

There is no real evidence the lighthouse draws people to jump but despite other access points to fatal heights all along the cliffs, many choose to die either side of it. Most jump to the east of the light which, mysteriously, forms a perfect triangle from the Beachy Head Pub to a straight line to the cliffs, 500m east. This area is aptly named 'Falling Sands'. Not through association with the jumpers, but because on a windless day, you will hear the sound of millions of tiny chalk grains as they roll down the cliff face to the shingle beach below.

The triangle is made perfect by a straight line drawn south west from the lighthouse, crossing the cliff top at 300m. It is within this triangle that the majority of suicides occur. Perhaps there is a biblical, spiritual magnetism that tempts people in an unconscious re-creation of the fate of Cain who was 'cursed from the earth', cast out from the presence of the Lord and banished to the East of Eden. At the Golden Gate Bridge in San Francisco most of the suicides from the bridge also happen on the east side walkway within direct view of the lighthouse. (endnote: Genesis 4:1-16)

Beachy Head sheer view. © K. J. Varney

Knowing that many return to the spot, repeatedly, before actually going over the edge, perhaps the lighthouse is something to aim at, or provides comfort as a silent witness. In Sally Bedell Smith's biography *Portrait of a Troubled Princess,* she claims that Princess Diana returned many times to the windswept cliff top to contemplate suicide, but the thought of her sons deterred her from the final act.

But there is no denying the hypnotic effects this place has. Louis de Bernieres, (author of *Captain Corelli's Mandolin*) had the same experience when he happened upon Beachy Head in 1995: 'Several times I went up to the edge in order to look down, and in every instance I was overwhelmed by an unconquerable nausea,' He could only admire the view while lying face down 10 ft from the peak, his white knuckles buried into the soil for fear of what may happen if he stood too close to the edge. He continues: 'Each time I approached the edge, I felt myself drawn over; the vertical became the horizontal, and a terrifying sickness took me at the stomach and throat. I have never felt this anywhere else, even when mountaineering or when I was a tree surgeon, and I wondered how many people might have been hypnotized into committing suicide unintentionally: this beautiful place invites you to die.' (endnote: Bernieres L D *Legends of the Fall* Harpers Magazine 1996)

Psychiatrists, academics, coastguards and concerned locals have long debated why this place of such outstanding beauty has such a tragic allure. In a recent documentary, director/producer Eric Steel tried to address this same question with regards to the Golden Gate Bridge. Steel had been inspired by an article he had read in *The New Yorker* by Tad Friend, called 'Jumpers', which highlighted the tragic stories of suicide from the bridge. Steel decided to make a documentary film that followed the controversial events on the bridge for a year. The film *The Bridge* was released in 2006 despite outcries from media watchdogs.

In his review of the finished piece, Eric is clearly moved by the awesome power of what drives someone to commit suicide so publicly: 'There is an eerie logic in selecting a means that is almost always fatal and a place that is magically, mysteriously beautiful.......I thought if I stared at the Golden Gate Bridge long enough, I might crack the code, understand its fatal beauty.'(endnote: The Bridge www.thebridge-themovie.com)

Chapter 13

Theories about suicide

Theories expound about the reasons why people commit suicide. Some experts write that mostly there are mental health issues to take into consideration, whilst others think that emotional conflict, hopelessness and learned behaviour are triggers, while others believe that the weather may be a contributing factor.

For example, in his experience, Mark Sawyer (RNLI), is strongly convinced that most of the suicides happen on Bank Holiday weekends, and he is certainly busier from April through to September: 'It seems the more stunning and peaceful the view the more likely they are to jump, I think it so closely resembles a heavenly place that they must feel is the most perfect place to die.'

Al Alvarez, British literary critic, writer and editor, also observes this in his classic work on suicide *The Savage God:* 'The cycle of self-destruction follows precisely that of nature: it declines in autumn, reaches its low in mid-winter and then begins to rise slowly with the sap; its climax is in early summer, May and June; in July it gradually begins once more to drop.' (endnote: *The Savage God* A. Alvarez first pub 1971 Random House GB)

Birling Gap. © R. Wassell

Historically, this seems to be true, On a gloriously warm April in 2007, five people, including two on the same day, decided to end their lives at the cliffs. Similarly, in May 2008, when the sun made a rare luminous appearance in an otherwise wet summer, eight people perished in that month alone.

The London Institute of Psychiatry carried out a detailed research over an 11-year period (1993-2003) to investigate if there was any truth in this theory. The results will surely raise a new dimension to the climate change debate. Dr Lisa Page concluded that suicide rates rise significantly when the average daily temperatures reach 18°C. During the period of study there were 53, 623 suicides in England and Wales equating to 13.3 per day; on 222 of those days the temperature rose above 18°C. When this happened the suicide rate increased by almost 4%. For violent deaths the figure was even higher at 5%. This issue of climate change must be seriously taken into consideration. The shocking facts are that during the 1995 heatwave, while most of us were enjoying the splendid weather, the forlorn, for unknown reasons, decided it was, indeed, the most beautiful day to die; the suicide rates for that glorious summer rose by 46.9%. (endnote: BBC NEWS Suicide rate rises in hot weather. Pub 01/08/07
http://news.bbc.co.uk/archives).

The most common month for suicides in 2007, at Beachy Head, was April; the warmest and driest on record in Eastbourne. Two of the five deaths for that month were on the 15th when the temperature was at its warmest 24.0°C. In October 2007, the Halifax Quality of Life Survey named Eastbourne as the sunniest place in Great Britain. For 2008, May carried on that burden with eight deaths recorded, four of which were in the same week, as the weather simmered at over 18.0C. But a detailed report by Dr John Surtees, a now retired clinical pathologist at Eastbourne District General Hospital, examining deaths over a much longer period (1965-1989), showed that June, July and August were the most common months to die, tailing off to less than half in January and February. (endnote: 1997 Beachy Head Surtees J SB Publications East Sussex).

	Jan	Feb	March	April	May	June	July	Aug	Sept	Oct	Nov	Dec
2007	3	3	0	5	2	4	0	3	2	2	2	1
2008	1	1	2	2	8	3	1	2	2	1	2	2
2009	1	1	2	2	5	2	2	1	4	1	2	1
1965 -1989	10	12	24	11	25	27	27	34	23	20	19	17

Others attribute suicide to the overwhelming power of nature. Dion Fortune (1891-1946), writer, pioneer psychologist, and powerful mystic was the founder of The Society of the Inner Light. In her book *Psychic Self -Defence* she talks of a terror when the grandeur of nature overwhelms even the most experienced mountaineers, oppressing their spirits. She felt it herself when

View from the headland. © K. J. Varney

she was visiting a hilltop overlooking the ocean calling her theory the Abyss of Height:

'I have already noted my exceptionally bad head for heights. I have found that it is considerably mitigated, temporarily at any rate, by the Invocation of Air. I am of the opinion that the curious impulse which causes people for no reason whatsoever to commit suicide by throwing themselves from heights may be due to the same impulse that causes people who are obsessed by the Element of Water to swim out to sea. These apparently causeless suicides by Water and Air are, in my opinion, a form of union with God which is one of the ideas underlying human sacrifice.'

She terms this 'juggernaut pang' and when it touched her that day she was advised by her celestial guides to go back to the cliffs and get into sympathetic touch with the Sylphs. It was a radiant day with the wind dancing high above. As she stood with her arms raised in invocation of the elemental kingdoms (Air, Water, Fire and Earth) the air appeared to be filled with silver sparkles telling her that the veil between her and the archangels was thin. A friend with her suddenly felt a sudden rush of power and began running headlong up the cliff. At the same time they both started dervishly dancing, revolving on their own axis, the air with the sun revolving around them conjuring rushing golden flames, lying level with the wind. Fortune claims that for days after, they were charged with elemental energy: 'I have never known a more

Downs and Beachy Head. © R. Wassell

Rugged cliff. © K. J. Varney

glorious experience.' (endnote: (2001) Fortune D. *Psychic Self-Defence* New Edition Red Wheel/WeriserBoston MA)

At Beachy Head, maybe, for one reflective moment, the power of nature may succeed in deterring the determined: one life saved, destiny altered. No one can truly know. Suicide is a solitary act explained by those that can never know what it ultimately feels like to take the final step, to abandon life completely, never to return to tell the tale. Emile Durkheim in his book *Suicide A study of suicidology* cites French poet, Larmartine's, famous work 'Raphael' as a reflection on melancholic suicide:

'The languor of all my surroundings was in marvellous harmony with my own languor. It increased this languor by its charm. I plunged into the depths of melancholy, full enough of thoughts, impressions, communings with the infinite, half-obscurity of my own soul, so that I had no wish to abandon it. A human disease, but one the experience of which attracts rather than pains, where death resembles a voluptuous lapse into the infinite. I resolved to abandon myself to it wholly, henceforth; to avoid all distracting society and to wrap myself in silence, solitude and frigidity in the midst of whatever company I should encounter; my spiritual isolation was a shroud, through which I desired no longer to see men, but only nature and God.'

Similarly, there are theories that explore the effects of certain surroundings on unstable minds. In Japan the government was so concerned with the increasing numbers of suicides on the railway system that they have introduced soothing music on all station platforms hoping to pacify any would-be jumpers into a reflective, positive mood hoping it may deter them.

Perhaps it is the trapped aura of all who have gone before, luring the 'weak to follow' Friedrich Engels and Karl Marx who were well known and frequent visitors to Beachy Head; as a dying wish Engels requested his friend Karl

Marx's wife to throw his ashes from the cliff top. Just before his death in August1895 Engels insisted that depressed individuals would regularly try and join him by leaping to their death from the then already notorious suicide spot.

In 2002 the government implemented a National Suicide Prevention Strategy (NSPS) for England. It is a comprehensive paper aimed at reducing the number of suicides by 20% by 2010. It covers everything that might cause an individual to commit suicide and examines topics such as age and gender vulnerability, mental health services, media coverage, the treatment of bereaved survivors and different methods used.

More detailed research reports focus on reducing the high amount of young men who kill themselves, and also look at 'high risk' occupation groups, such as farmers.

Gender is an issue for statistics, but not race. Neither the Office for National Statistics, Mind, or the Samaritans can pinpoint if white males are at the highest risk of suicide. Marital and geographical status, occupation and age dominate the analysis with some references made to the increase in the suicide rates of Asian women.

Data taken from intensive research conducted by Professor David Gunnell and Dr M Powers on *Suicide from the Clifton Suspension Bridge in England,* that the most likely time of day to commit suicide is reportedly between 10am and 6pm.(endnote: Suicide from the Clifton Suspension Bridge in England *Journal of Epidemiology and Community Health 1996:50:30-32* Gunnell D and Nowers M)

Most suicides happen at Beachy Head on the glorious dawn of the day as the sun rises on the distant horizon.

Chapter 14

The Media

John Surtees, who has keenly followed the deaths at the troubled cliffs for over 30 years, published his findings in January 2008 in the local Sussex newspaper. He made the headlines, just one week after Christmas, with 'Beachy Head deaths triple' by announcing that 18 people had plunged to their deaths in 2007 compared to seven in the previous year. It was woefully under the actual figures and the article wrongly attributed the increase in suicides to the fact that Keith Lane had decided to end his vigil on the cliff top.

So is the media to blame? Does it have a moral responsibility for suicide prevention? Are we, as a society, really so entrenched in strangers' lives that we would mimic their chosen method of death and suffer the same fate? Every academic in the field has reviewed data after data from fictional characters on TV, film, and stage to classic poetry to front page headlines going back as early as the 18th century.

The possibilities of imitation or 'copycat' suicides were first considered after the publication of *The Sorrows of Young Werther* in 1774. The plot of the novel follows the hero through a tempestuous love affair ending with his dramatic death by shooting himself in the head. The author, Goethe, was vilified for portraying suicide as sentimental and was accused by coroners across Europe of creating what became known as the 'Werther effect' or 'copycat' suicides in young people. But it also had the effect of creating an empathy with suicide, lifting it from its reputation as a revolting, hideous act against God and man to a more emotional tragedy. He also inspired many writers to openly address the taboo subject.

More recently, there was heightened anticipation of a plot on the BBC soap *Eastenders* when the character Angie was about to confront her husband, nicknamed 'Dirty Den', about an affair she had recently discovered. 14 million people in the UK tuned in on Thursday 27th February 1986 with another nine million watching the Omnibus edition the following Sunday. The viewers already knew that Den was a love cheat and were on the edge of their seats to see what Angie would do when she finally confronted him. The build up involved scenes of Angie buying several bottles of aspirin and gin in a catastrophic emotional state.

The act of attempted suicide was never actually shown but strongly intimated. After the episodes were screened two London hospitals, Hackney Hospital and St Bartholomew's Hospital, reported large numbers of admissions to the Accident and Emergency departments, where people had taken overdoses. Hackney, in particular, sent an alarming letter to the *Lancet* medical magazine, claiming: 'That week was far in excess of the average for the previous ten weeks, and of the average for that week for six out of the previous ten years.'

Beachy Head. © K. J. Varney

On closer examination, Professor Mark Williams, (Professor of Clinical psychology, University of Oxford - Centre for Suicide Research) carried out research on the two London hospitals, and concluded that there was no evidence to suggest that there had been a copycat effect from this show. He examined data for the period up to and including the dates of the broadcast and compared them to two control years. Although there was an increase in the numbers of attendances at the casualty department from drug overdose at these two hospitals, it was found that the increases had, in fact, begun some two months before the broadcast in December in one hospital and January in the other. (endnote: Williams M *Suicide and attempted suicide* Penguin London First published 1997)

A separate survey of 63 hospitals across the country was also carried out which found that the cases of attempted suicide by overdosing in London were lower, despite having the highest viewing figures of *Eastenders,* than hospitals in Yorkshire and the northeast, which had the lowest numbers of viewers tuning in.

So does 'Werther' still hover in the minds of those most in crisis? According to the Samaritans he clearly does. In their media guidelines they cite an episode of the popular medical drama *Casualty* where there was a scene of one of the patients overdosing using over-the-counter drugs.

'Research showed that self-poisoning increased by 17% in the week following the broadcast and by 9% in the second week using the same drug. 20% of self-poisoning patients who had seen the programme said that it had influenced their decision to commit suicide.' (endnote: Samaritans. Media guidelines. How does drama affect suicide rates? www.samaritans.org/media_centre/media_guidelines.aspx)

In Germany, the series *Death of a Student* began each episode with the scene of a young man dying by placing himself on a railway line. This was directly linked to a staggering increase of 175%, concerning young men who chose to die by the very same violent method. As all research models are cloaked in difficulties and controversy, a theme as complex to navigate as suicide prevention will, inevitably, lead any series editor to follow cautionary guidelines. All media watchdogs and professional bodies embrace, with respect, the Samaritans' advice to write sensitive, intelligent articles and storylines. But how do they truly balance that with public curiosity on taboo subjects?

In the Sussex local papers not all deaths at Beachy Head are reported but when they are they always feature at the top spot on the 'Most read stories' column. In San Francisco, in 1973, local papers the *Chronicle*, and the *Examiner* began a public countdown as to who would be the 500th person to jump from the Golden Gate Bridge. As the numbers rose, bridge officials stepped up their vigilance, saving 14 people from going over the edge, including one who had pinned a sign with '500' on his T-shirt.

By 1995 the figure had approached 1000, creating even more of a frenzy. A local disc jockey even went as far as offering a case of Snapple to the family of the 1000th 'victim'. In June of that year, in a desperate bid to stop the promotion of self-sacrifice, the California Highway Patrol put a stop to their official count at 997. It was inevitable that someone would become the 1000th statistic. That sad accolade went to a 25-year-old man who was seen to jump although his body was never recovered, no doubt washed out to the Pacific Ocean and lost forever.

Why is suicide the only fearful act that is singled out?

Front page headlines never shy away from publishing every detail of child abduction or brutal murders. In fact more than twice as many people die from suicide than they do from murder in America even with the global adherence to suicide reporting.

Eric Steele, having filmed a year of activity at the Golden Gate Bridge, confirms the hushed attitude to suicide: 'In the United States there are almost twice as many suicides each year than homicides. While homicides are a nightly recitation on the local news, suicides are rarely mentioned.'

It significantly remains a dreadful fate too terrible to discuss openly in all forms of the media unless it involves a high profile 'celebrity' or what is commonly termed suicide clusters. 'Bills' Reg slashes wrists' on January 9th 2008, 'It would be better if I was dead. Britney's heartbreaking suicide note.' January 16th - the tabloid newspapers increasingly reveal every detail of spiralling, celebrity depression.

In San Francisco, the Bay Area media also restrict their reporting to only include jumpers who are celebrities or if the incident is causing traffic chaos. Coroner Ken Holmes in 2003 summed up the reality for the entire world's media to consider; having 'weaned' the press away from sensational reporting he stated: 'The lack of publicity hasn't reduced the number of suicides at all.' It seems he is tragically right, on January 9th 2008 on the bridge rail website he published a press release, it made for very grim reading 'Gate Bridge Suicide Death Toll: At Least 35 in 2007-' (endnote: The Bridge Rail Foundation. Press release Gate Bridge Suicide Death Toll: At Least 35 in 2007- www.bridgerail.org).

On June 2nd 2009 daily newspapers reported the grim discovery of two bodies at the foot of Beachy Head on the balmy Sunday evening of May 31st. This tragic story made headlines because when Stuart McNab made the descent the following morning to recover the bodies, he also discovered two rucksacks strewn on the shore. Carefully opening them he found one containing a child's toys; in the other was the tiny broken body of a five-year-old boy. By June 3rd the story was front page news across the world. Devoted parents, Neil and Kazumi Puttick had taken their disabled son, who had sadly passed away on the previous Friday, on their final family trip. With his body inside a rucksack the couple drove 120 miles from their Wiltshire home, abandoned their car and jumped together from the highest point of the cliffs just east of the lighthouse. It was a heartbreaking story of despair. The media recorded every detail. One copycat attempt was averted on the following Tuesday when police, acting on a tip off, intercepted a man driving with his two children to the same spot. Apart from that incident, despite fears of attracting an increase in deaths at Beachy Head, there have, in fact, been fewer suicides for the following six months than the previous two years.

The media report unusual deaths as headline news and take the brunt of the blame for any apparent 'copycat' deaths, but without the widespread awareness the tragic consequences of suicide on families and communities will continue to fester. At Bridgend, a small town on the edge of a South Wales valley, 25 young people have killed themselves in 23 months since January 2007. As the news travelled around the world, all eyes focused on this tiny corner of Britain. Only then did the Welsh government set up a suicide prevention strategy aimed at reducing the suicide rate by 10% in four years. Despite the fact that the suicide rate in Wales was already way above average at 21 suicides per 100,000 population.

When the lust for news of these teenage deaths reached a peak the sudden focus of blame fell on the new media of the Internet. Pro-suicide sites were rightly vilified, yet social networking sites such as Bebo and Facebook were also put in the frame as teenagers expressed their mourning as tender memorials to the dead. Yet it is widely acknowledged that young men, in particular, have difficulty expressing themselves, often isolated in society's 'big boys don't cry' mentality. Just maybe these sites offer an outlet, allowing them to utter the words or thoughts held most deeply in the heart, giving them a sense of belonging, a shared sorrow.

Kitch and Hume, in their introduction to the book *Journalism in a Culture of Grief,* explain: 'News reports about death carry a special authority. Because they are based on fact - on real people who die in real circumstances and real people who mourn them - they seem to have an authenticity and transparency, an evident "truth," even as they perform ritual processes of tribute and commemoration. They also create a sense of intimacy and inclusion, allowing a broader audience to mourn along with the central characters, even to feel they are somehow part of a private ceremony.' (endnote: 2008 *Journalism in a Culture of Grief* Routledge UK).

Derek Christie on descent.
© H.M. Coastguard

The fear that ravaged though the town of Bridgend was strangely assigned to 'cops,' in news reports stating that the police were associating the deaths with a 'macabre fame' syndrome undermining the professionalism of the police and the depth of despair qualified merely to a celebrity obsessive culture. The deaths at Bridgend were needless, tragic wastes of young lives but needed to be reported; it is inevitably the quality of such reporting that is the key to breaking the 'taboo'. Calling these events clusters or 'copy-cat' suicides sends a message that they are somehow linked, drawing the vulnerable to imitate. The research for this is variable and controversial.

Thomas Joiner, clinical psychologist and author of *Why people die by suicide* offering analysis on a small community in Northern Ireland where three 15-year-old boys from the same school all committed suicide within three weeks of each other recorded: 'This agonizing phenomenon is known as a "suicide cluster," an event in which these deaths gather in space and time, beyond what would be expected ordinarily. The phrase "beyond what would be expected ordinarily" is important, because suicides are not equally distributed in time and space, and thus apparent clusters can sometimes be explained with reference to mundane factors such as time of year and country of residence. In the northern hemisphere, most deaths by suicide occur in late spring and early summer, as these did - not during the winter holiday season as commonly believed, which in fact represents the time when the fewest suicides occur. The geographical distribution of suicides is also not random; there is some evidence that Northern Ireland has an above-average rate.' All indications according to Thomas Joiner therefore point to a suicide cluster. (endnote: Together in life and death. Timesonline *The Times* June 21 2007)

Yet at Bridgend only a handful of the 25 deaths were considered a suicide cluster based on the fact that they all knew one another. The others were attributed to a learned fearlessness to the act of hanging, or from reading the reports in the local and national media, and acting on suicidal feelings that are already harbouring in the mind of those feeling most hopeless. This perceived hopelessness is a stark warning; suicide will always tarnish society with its futility but countless lives could be saved.

There is no point meeting them on the precipice, too many return. The only method of prevention that will truly achieve is to empower people with a sense of worth, a positive community involvement, a fulfilment of feeling needed and realistic aspiration. This cannot always be achieved at home; loving parents are burdened with the why and the guilt. It is a new world that needs new tactics, not easily fixed with a pill or psychiatry. It is no coincidence that when society pulls together, such as times of war, the suicide rate reduces. Social networking sites encourage peers, of all ages, to communicate, whether through joy or mourning, trying to connect with people who seem also to be lost in a global secret of which they have no access. Rites of passage must be re-established, in particular, for the young, white males who have, for too long, been the forgotten souls on the early path to heaven.

Suicide at Beachy Head is not considered a cluster, maybe because it is so acceptable that it is no longer considered 'beyond what would be expected ordinarily' and that only 32% of the deaths are by people from the local area. But it is the truth, so rarely spoken; suicide exists, suicide among the white population is pandemic and Beachy Head is a beautiful, lethal magic that draws them with each rising sun.

Chapter 15

Murder, Crime and Investigation

So what happens when the evidence is far more sinister? How easy is it to prove suicide as murder? Is it not the most perfect crime? To wait in the dark of night, a gentle stroll under the moonlight, no witness, no murder weapon, no clues. A slight nudge of the shoulder or subtle push; even evidence of a violent shove would be lost on the broken remains on the boulder beach below.

Was that the fate of Paula Ramsden, age 32, on January 9th 2000? When Paula first met 38-year-old Paul Ramsden she was already a mother of two to Daniel and Michelle. Happy pictures of the couple were featured in a local news report, enjoying a holiday in 1993. The report also carried the tragic details of Paula's sudden death at the foot of the cliffs at Beachy Head. Yet on that fateful day the truth was a solemn foe. Paul told the story that, one evening, he and his wife had left their home in Crawley Downs to take a romantic stroll on the headland (friends and relatives would later claim that Paula was terrified of heights.) At the inquest Paul described that they had stood on the cliff edge, kissing and cuddling, when suddenly Paula 'turned and fell.' Paul was, at the time, working as an Operations Manager for Shell UK. It was there he met, and began a love affair, with a colleague. During months of exhaustive investigations, Sussex police were hoping for a breakthrough from a 'third party'. Possibly meaning the 'other woman'.

They knew that Mr Ramsden had renewed a life insurance policy on his wife from 1994, then worth £104,000, to a new pay out of £225,000 just a few months before her death. He was quickly arrested. Alan Craze, in charge of the inquest went on record as saying: 'The inquest has been like a murder trial but there's no prosecution. If a 100 people had been asked - 'Do you believe he killed his wife?' - a very considerable number would say yes. In my judgment he would have been capable of doing so. He has shown to be dishonest, egocentric, manipulative and a control freak.' He concluded: 'I have to decide whether it's been proven on the evidence that he did so. There is plenty of evidence, mostly circumstantial, which would show he had a motive. If he did not do it the death was a huge coincidence.' Mr Craze returned an open verdict. (endnote: New evidence in death plunge case. BBC NEWS 15/04/2002 http://news.bbc.co.uk/archives *BBC NEWS* 21/04/02 http://news.bbc.co.uk/archives)

In his defence, Paul Ramsden stated: 'I did not push her off. It was not coming to an end - me and Paula were on top of the world.' He stated later: 'My life is completely ruined by the tragic loss of my wife. I did not murder her. I loved her.'

Ramsden continued to reject suggestions that he had wilfully pushed his wife to her death to collect the life insurance and begin a new life with his mistress, Liz Harrison. Detective Inspector Tim Guyton, leading the investigation was at a loss: 'There will be no new inquiry unless we receive new information. There is no way any more can come from what happened on the top of Beachy Head that night because only two people really know. One is gone and the other, Paul Ramsden, is sticking to his guns.'

Paul Ramsden was released from custody without charge with a promise that Paula's life insurance pay out would go to her children. Eight years later they are still waiting. In 2006 his wife's family contacted a Sunday newspaper to say that they had still not received a penny.

Are there other 'murder' victims haunting the headland? In 1989 Sussex police were called to Beachy Head after the grisly discovery of human remains hidden in the undergrowth. The area was quickly sealed off for forensic pathologists to examine the vicinity. It didn't take long to determine that the body was missing art student, Jessie Earl, 22.

In 1980, having just finished her exams, Jessie had walked from her bed-sit in Eastbourne to the local phone box to call her mother to say she was coming home for the weekend. For nine years, her parents, John and Valerie waited for the knock on the door. When that knock finally came it wasn't Jessie standing on the porch, it was the Sussex police, bringing them the news that their only daughter was dead. She had lain undiscovered in a shallow grave, naked for all that time. The only piece of clothing recovered was her bra which had been used to tie her wrists together, although there were no other signs of violence. John and Valerie knew in their hearts that their daughter had been murdered yet the coroner, at the time, returned an open verdict. The trail was cold.

It wasn't until 21 years later, in March 2000 that Sussex police re-opened the case after it was featured on BBC's *Crimewatch* programme. In the hope that an appeal would bring forward new evidence, they decided to try a new tactic and enlisted the help of the Eastbourne and District Metal Detector Club. Together with an archaeological pathologist, they combed the area looking for clues. An incident room was set up at Eastbourne police station and scientists worked tirelessly at the National Crime Faculty at Bramshill, Hampshire. On the 16th December the exhaustive hunt was once again called off. That was until the discovery of the body of a Polish student in Margate.

Police arrested local man Peter Tobin on suspicion of murder. His macabre history soon unraveled. For 40 years Tobin had left behind him a bloody trail of young girls all across the United Kingdom. As Tobin had lived locally to Eastbourne, he was now a prime suspect in the murder of Jessie Earl. Tobin was sentenced to life in May 2007, without making any sort of confession, leaving police across the country still investigating a link to 15 other murders. Jessie's remains may have never been found but a body that was clearly meant to be found was discovered in 2004.

It was a dull, drizzly Friday afternoon in January when the Sussex police helicopter flew routinely over the cliffs at Beachy Head looking for anything suspicious. It was just past 3pm when the pilot, dipping the blades to get closer to the cliff face, noticed what looked to be a body on the rocks below. Turning to fly past again he was horrified to see what appeared to be three more bodies all lying within 50 ft of each other. The coastguards were immediately alerted and raced to the cliff top but were driven back by treacherous weather.

Early Saturday morning, just as daylight broke, a full team of volunteers were once again harnessed, ready to ascend the cliffs. The inshore lifeboat was being buffeted on the wintry sea a few hundred yards out caught in the downwind of the hovering helicopter which was patiently waiting to carry the bodies inland. When the cliff rescue team reached the beach, they walked the slippery rocks, examining each body as they came across them. On crackling radios they relayed the message to Dover coastguard control that they had discovered three bodies, not four as first reported. One had been ripped in half. Two of the victims were thought to be possible suicides that had gone over the cliffs at different times as their smashed remains were at different stages of decomposition. But one was disturbingly different. Once the other two bodies had been retrieved, detectives were called to investigate what was to become a murder scene.

On closer examination they quickly realised that the unknown man had been savagely attacked before he had even reached the shingle beach. Both his hands and legs were bound and a plastic bag was tightly secured over his head. He was described by Sussex Police Detective Chief Inspector Tony O' Donnell, leading the case, as 'Black, aged around 30, 5ft 8in tall, with a full Afro hairstyle and a full black beard. He was of slim, athletic build and wore a Performance-wear coat, black Groove Armada zip-up top and blue jeans.' Close to the body was a 220-litre (50 gallon) blue plastic barrel, 3ft high and 2ft wide. The police soon had good reason for suspecting foul play. Local coastguards and lifeboat crews regularly search and remove any unknown

Meagre fence not deterring a popular suicide spot. © K. J. Varney

debris from the beach so they were able to confirm that the barrel had not been there previously. The police came to the grisly conclusion that the barrel may have been used to hold the dead body, and was then rolled over the cliff top. Police quickly removed the barrel for detailed analysis of fingerprints, DNA, or body fluids. Forensic evidence conducted by the Home Office Pathologist revealed later that the man had died from multiple stab wounds. Detectives appealed for witnesses, but none came forward.

Operation Dundee was now launched. O'Donnell, believing that the victim had been killed midweek prior to its discovery and dumped at the cliffs any time after Tuesday launched a statement: 'He has certainly been subjected to a savage attack, and his body brought to Beachy Head and dumped. My priorities are to identify both the victim and the murder scene. It could well have been a flat somewhere and he may have been placed in the barrel where he died. There will have been a great deal of blood there.' (endnote: *Eastbourne Herald* Gagged and Bound: Beachy Head Murder Hunt. Pub 21/01/04).

By 4th March 2004, police had made an important breakthrough. Blood samples taken from the victim during a postmortem examination matched splashes of blood found at an empty restaurant. It was a popular takeaway in the south London district of Brixton. O' Donnell said after the discovery: 'We believe that our victim possibly came from the south London area and now this confirms this to us. We believe he was living in the area. We need to know his name - I believe that people out there must know him. Someone must be missing him.'

The police offered no clues as to how they were led to discover the 'fair sized' pool of blood that had stained a chair at the back of Hellshire Chat-Bout Jamaican Best Food Takeaway in Loughborough Road, but did reveal that they had found the evidence as a result of a random warrant on the premises on 17th February for an unrelated matter. The restaurant had been empty since January. All the evidence indicated that the victim had been stabbed almost to death in the empty building, then gagged, trussed and bundled into a car and driven to Beachy Head, where he was thrown over the cliff.

With no definite motive, O'Donnell could only speculate: 'We do know that our victim was a frequent cocaine user. It may well be that drugs are a possible motive for this.' (endnote: *Independent.co.uk* Murder hunt begins after three bodies are found at Beachy Head. Pub 18/01/04 Sophie Goodchild)

By the 8th of March police had identified the victim: a 39-year-old Jamaican man, Orville Donovan Gordon, thought to have been previously living in Brixton. They suspected that his death was a savage revenge attack for a robbery that he had possibly committed. One 34-year-old man was arrested then released on bail, but three other suspects fled the country.

It was to be a busy year for Sussex detectives. By the end of April detectives had another death to investigate. On August 11th 2003, single mum, Paige Tapp, age 23, of Salehurst Road, Eastbourne, went to Beachy Head with every intention of plunging from the cliffs. A female officer, PC Sasha Coote, was on duty when the call came in from the coastguards that someone was acting suspiciously on the headland. When PC Coote arrived, she found Paige sitting on the edge of the cliff. The police officer already knew Paige as she was often in trouble with the police and had previously received a 12-month conditional discharge for making nuisance calls to the emergency services. However, the police officer wasn't aware that the young mum's children had just been taken into the care of social services.

As the distraught woman sat with her legs dangling over the edge, she started to shout that she was going to jump, adding a chilling threat: 'I hate that bitch P.C. Coote. I hate her. Do you know what I am going to do next, next time she talks to me? I am going to grab her and drag her over the edge with me.'

Undaunted, Coote put on a safety harness and moved closer to the edge towards Paige. With patient negotiation she managed to talk the depressed woman away from the cliff. Next day Paige continued to make menacing threats to psychiatric nurses during her assessment before being discharged from hospital where she was sent back to her empty home.

Three days later she returned to Beachy Head. Police were once again called when witnesses reported seeing a woman running towards the lighthouse. The wind was unusually strong for the time of year and could easily have carried her over the cliffs. When help arrived Paige hadn't gone over the edge but was sitting directly opposite the red and white lighthouse, the beam just beginning to faintly penetrate the falling dusk sky. PC Coote was advised to keep back this time as Paige gave her a chilling warning: 'Do you know what I really want to do? I want to have PC Coote with me and take her off the edge with me. I hate her.'

Somehow she was calmed down enough for other police officers to get her off the headland and was taken to the local police station. Paige was remanded in custody for her own protection until a court date was set for a Monday morning in March 2004 at Hove crown court. Prosecutor Richard Keogh on cross-examination was curious as to why the defendant had taken such a strong dislike to the police officer. Paige replied 'She stopped me from killing myself and swore at me.' His response to the jury was: 'If Miss Tapp had genuinely wanted to die by now she would have self-harmed enough and put herself in such situations to make death inevitable. What the events at Beachy Head are in essence are cries for help by somebody who has nobody in life.' (endnote: *Eastbourne Herald* Jail for mum who made death threats. Pub24/03/04)

Paige was sentenced to two years imprisonment by Judge Anthony Niblett and sent to Send prison in Surrey. One month into her sentence, prison officers entered her cell at 3pm on a Sunday afternoon, and found the young mum hanging from a crude noose made from her bed linen. An ambulance was called, but despite every effort, she was pronounced dead on arrival at the Royal Sussex County Hospital.

For years Beachy Head has been the scene of murder and attempted murder. In May 2007 (followed by a Channel 4 documentary in 2008 *The girls who were found alive*) the world's news reported the terrible case of two young friends, Charlene Lunnon and Lisa Hoodless. After eight years the two young women, deciding to waive their anonymity, spoke for the first time about their terrible kidnap ordeal in the filthy hands of a known paedophile.

On January 19th 1999 the two little girls met as usual for the walk to primary school. As they played on the journey they suddenly noticed a scruffy man opening the boot of his car. As they hurriedly tried to pass him, Alan Hopkinson, then 45, suddenly grabbed Lisa by the face; Charlene wanted to run but was afraid for her friend. Hopkinson scooped her from the pavement too, throwing her into the boot next to Lisa, slamming it shut. The next three days were a horrifying ordeal for the 10-year-olds as they were separately subjected to terror and sexual abuse.

As the days went on Hopkinson became more and more agitated; he had already served seven years for the abduction and abuse of an 11-year-old girl. As the police net closed he made a terrifying decision, and their ordeal took a horrible twist. Bundling them, once again, into the boot of his car, one in a bin liner and the other in a sports holdall, he drove from his dingy flat above a shopping precinct in Eastbourne to the cliffs of Beachy Head. He later told police that he was planning to throw them to their deaths. As a wintry dusk shrouded the headland nobody heard their screams. Hopkinson cruelly dangled them like rag dolls over the cliff edge. Charlene recalls:

'He was hanging us over the edge. I remember him holding us off the cliff. He said he was going to kill us. We both gave up hope and thought this is it now. We just gave up. By this time we were too messed up. There were no feelings, no emotions. Then he said "No, I want you for one more day."'

Hiding them once again, he drove them back to the squalid flat. On the fourth day, by pure chance following up a separate allegation, the police knocked on the door. At first Hopkinson ignored their insistent hammering, as the girls sat, waiting in hope, in the front room. Eventually, he opened the door; knowing they would now make the discovery he confessed to the officers about the girls and led them to the room. Hopkinson is now serving nine life sentences. The girls have finally had the courage to revisit Beachy Head, speaking out for the first time to help promote Sarah's Law, a campaign set up after the tragic death of 8-year-old Sarah Payne at the hands of a known paedophile. It aims to give parents the right to gain access to the whereabouts of known sex offenders in their area and to protect other innocent children. (endnote: *News of the World* 27/05/07 Rape beast kidnapper dangled us over edge of Beachy Head).

In May 2006, 60-year-old Dennis Wimpory left his home in Maidenhead and drove straight to the cliffs of Beachy Head. Once there, he abandoned his car and hurled himself to the rocks below. He had been sinking into depression due to the recent break up of his 34-year marriage to his 57-year-old wife, Jean. His daughter told the coroner that just three days before he had phoned her stating that he had travelled to Beachy Head to see if he had the courage to throw himself off. Just days later Jean convinced Dennis to see a doctor, and phoned their daughter to let her know that something was being done to help him. But it was to no avail. Police traced the registration of the car to the couple's home.

When the police arrived to inform Jean about her husband's death, they made another grim discovery. As they forced their way into the front room they found Jean lying face down in a pool of blood. She had been stabbed five times in the neck with a six-inch knife. The coroner recorded a verdict of suicide and one of unlawful killing.

How many others that have perished at Beachy Head by the sinister hands of another will never be known.

Chapter 16

Making the verdict

When the book *Beachy Head* was published in 1997 by John Surtees, a clinical pathologist for Eastbourne General Hospital, and leading expert on suicide by jumping at Beachy Head, there was one suicide in England and Wales every three hours. In 2002 when the government introduced the National Suicidal Prevention Strategy for England, (NSPS) the figure was one every two hours. That identifiable statistic now stands at one suicide every 88 minutes. Worldwide that figure is one every 40 seconds.

Professor Mark Williams explains the history of suicide in his book *Suicide and Attempted Suicide,* giving expert insight into society's view of the self-sacrificer by looking closely at how coroners made decisions in the past.

In the Middle Ages, Christian thinkers argued that suicide was a mortal and cardinal sin spurred on by Devil possession. Coroners and their pastoral juries were tasked with posthumous judgments over suicide victims. If they were convicted of murdering themselves *(felo de se)* all their worldly goods were forfeited to the Crown, reducing the family they left behind to abject poverty. The verdict also brought terrible shame on the family as the self-murderers were denied a Christian burial, banished in death from the consecrated ground of church cemeteries. Instead, their bodies were often buried naked at a crossroads with a wooden stake driven through the heart. When the shallow hole was filled in, the stake was left above the ground to remind passers-by of the shameful consequences of this chosen death.

Al Alvarez observes in his classic book on suicide *The Savage God:* 'The chosen site was usually a crossroads, which was also the place of public execution, and a stone was placed over the dead man's face; like the stake, it would prevent him rising as a ghost to haunt the living. Apparently, the terror of suicides lasted longer than the fear of vampires and witches.'

This meant that the juries, mostly made up of local people, were reluctant to bring a verdict of suicide, and would often look for evidence of insanity *(non compos mentis)* which allowed for a dignified burial, and saved the family from the pauper's life. By the 1600s, the Crown, dissatisfied with the numbers of verdicts of 'insanity' and the loss of revenue it entailed, tightened the laws and gave autonomy to the Court of Star Chamber to review and reform the terms of judgment. This led to a dramatic increase in the number of suicides reported to the King's Bench.

Later, the Church relented on the rituals of burial desecration, and a compromise was found that allowed the victims of self-murder to be buried in the churchyards. They were to have a place on the north side of the church alongside executed felons, excommunicates and unbaptised infants. But, by the late 18th century, burial spaces had become so scarce that the clergy had to, desperately, try to persuade families to take up plots next to these graves. But local communities were horrified, fearing that the land was polluted, and refused to have loved ones interned anywhere near the unconsecrated ground.

By 1870 Parliament acted to repeal the laws of 'profane burial' as it was deemed a brutal punishment for the living rather than the dead. The new ruling meant that victims of *felo de se* could now be buried in consecrated ground if the ceremony took place at night, but made no demands on the clergy to perform burial rites over the bodies. They also repealed the rights of the Crown to benefit from the worldly goods of felons and self-murderers. In a new twist, however, they also pronounced attempted suicide as a crime. In previous centuries, self-harmers were sent to madhouses, workhouses, or as a last resort to jails for their own protection, but now, all over Britain, they were arrested and often charged and interned as criminals. This did not change until Parliament again repealed the law as late as 1961.

Coroners no longer needed to attest to the sanity of anyone who had committed suicide, yet what is still considered the 'gravest taboo' torments their decisions. Records show that different coroners take a different view on what constitutes suicide. Mark Williams records: 'Usually a suicide note is considered the defining feature yet only a third of those that chose this death leave a note of any kind.' At Beachy Head, suicide notes are even more rarely found, so other circumstances are considered, as outlined by John Surtees in an article published in the *British Medical Journal:* 'The factors used to build up a suicide profile.' These factors are both general and then specific to Beachy Head.

General includes:
- Leaving a suicide note
- Previous suicide attempts
- History of mental illness
- Recent severe emotional upset
- Single marital state in an adult
- A medical consultation (probably for psychiatric reasons in previous three months)
- "High risk" occupation

Specific to Beachy Head includes:
- Being seen to jump or push off
- Suspicious behaviour at the cliff edge
- Leaving personal possessions on the cliff top
- Family history of suicide at Beachy Head
- Death within 14 days of a fatality at Beachy Head
- Domicile outside East Sussex
- Taking a taxi ride straight to Beachy Head

Since this article he has added in his book *Beachy Head* (1997)
- Leaving a suicide note (unambiguous)
- An act carried out in isolation with evidence of premeditation
- Previous suicide attempts (50% had carried out previous attempts)
- A history of mental disorder
- A patient in a psychiatric hospital
- Alcohol or drug problems
- Recent severe emotional upset
- A male over 45 living alone
- Consultation with their doctor for a psychiatric condition in previous three months

(endnote: Surtees S J *British Medical Journal* Volume 284 30/01/82 Medical Practice Occasional Review Suicide and accidental death at Beachy Head.)

Even when a suicide note has been left it is still open to interpretation and is critically scrutinised for its actual meaning. Did the author mean to die, either then or later, or was it a 'cry for help?' A desperate wish to be taken seriously with a governor's reprieve or an honest intent to choose to die? Declarations vary in expression, meaning and tone. Some are angry, hostile and full of blame whilst others may be remorseful or simply messages of farewell. Strangers pick at each word, analyse and make decisions as to the state of mind of the person who wrote it. How will this translate in the 21st century? Some suicidal intentions are being sent by text message to family and friends or declared publicly on internet web pages such as MySpace and Facebook. The mobile phone light, dimly illuminating a downcast face for a brief moment, then, without a second glance, they are gone, floating into the wind away from the cliff edge, slowly down to a lethal death. Seven seconds of life's harsh reality filling their final moments, before landing, broken on the shingle beach below. The final act of so many lost souls, reaching out for one last time with a simple text message, confirming their death wish: a most modern suicide note. In the *Irish Examiner* Tom Gillespie reported: 'People about to take their own lives are increasingly using text messages and voicemail instead of handwritten notes as a means of delivering chilling messages, a coroner revealed at the weekend.' He went on to quote, 'The coroner for South Mayo

John O'Dwyer said the use of mobile phones was becoming a common way of notifying family or friends.'

Evidence of a text message as a suicide note have not been recorded on the South Downs or openly acknowledged despite the Beachy Head Chaplaincy Team (BHCT) declaring that this is a definitive 21st century warning of the final act.

A verdict brings closure but what is the right verdict? Coroners have no guidelines, point of reference or formal expertise in clarifying intent from a suicide note or indeed a text message. Coroners can bring a narrative judgment where they make a brief and factual statement at the conclusion of an inquest but do not return one of the suggested short-form verdicts. It is unclear where that narrative judgment features in recording statistics. As independent judicial officers, they are currently employed, part-time on a pay scale of £100,000, by the local council, and are drawn mostly from the legal profession, by recommendation rather than through advertisement. They are also allowed to continue working in their own profession on full wages. Since the Harold Shipman case, where coroners received a backlash because of loopholes in the methods used for recording death certificates and cremation certificates which allowed Shipman's killing spree to go undetected for 23 years, coroners' roles have been under review. In 2006, the government published a Coroner's Draft Reform Bill; if successful through the House of Commons, it will acknowledge and redress the fact that (as stated in the foreword by Harriet Harman and Lord Falconer© Crown) 'The coroners' system is at present fragmented, non-accountable, variable in its processes and its quality, ineffective in part, archaic in its statutory basis and very much dependent on the good people working in or resourcing it, at present for its continued ability to respond to the demands we place upon it.'

The Coroner's Officers Association expressed their own concerns about the new bill and stated that the key role of the Coroner's Service was to protect society. Their doubts centred on the fact that 'The purpose of the current proposals is not to improve death reporting and investigation but to divert attention away from the deficiencies in the death certification process and the lack of scrutiny. Nothing in this Draft Bill would help detect or prevent another "Dr Shipman."' (endnote: Hurst Christine The Coroner's Officers Association response to the government's Draft Bill on Coroner's reform. Accessed 09/01/08 www.coronersofficer.org.uk

Many likely suicides have been recorded as open verdicts, accident or misadventure, making it difficult to define just how many people actually purposely perish at the foot of the cliffs. After many years of research, John Surtees conducted a comprehensive study on deaths at Beachy Head over the period 1965-1989. His research examined 250 total deaths with verdicts of 134 suicides, 100 open and 16 'other' (e.g. misadventure or accident) but the patterns remain true today. Different coroners appear to take differing views, as John Surtees notes: 'No single factor, apart from a recent proven suicide note, is sufficient to confirm suicide, but whereas none of the accident victims had even three of these suicide factors, all of the suicide verdicts had three or more, as did 97 of the 100 open verdicts, three of the seven misadventure and two of the three 'other' verdicts. Some victims of open verdicts had eight suicide factors.'

As an expert opinion he concluded that as many as 236 of the 250 deaths at the Beachy Head cliffs from 1965 to 1989 were suicides and, at Beachy Head, the coroner's verdicts were not necessarily indicative as to whether a death was suicide. (endnote: 1997 Surtees J. *Beachy Head* Appendix 2 S.B. Publications East Sussex)

In 1997, Chief Coroner for East Sussex, Mr Alan Craze, then acting as deputy coroner, returned an open verdict on a 25-year-old woman who had jumped from Beachy Head, despite a history of depression, previous suicide attempts, exam stress, and a boyfriend and sister who had committed suicide. When contacted in 2007, Mr Craze, now Chief Coroner for East Sussex, refused to discuss any issues relating to decisions he has since made regarding Beachy Head, claiming he has a strict rule never to speak to the press or researchers or 'pretty well anybody' about incidents or indeed the yearly number of actual deaths at the foot of Beachy Head.

Somehow this adds to the mystery, with coroners still making medieval decisions over the outcome, they also have autonomy over which records are designated for permanent preservation. The Remote Enquiries Manager for the National Archives explained: 'Records of reported deaths are closed for 75 years and any request to see closed records should be directed to the appropriate local coroner's office. A random sample of other papers may also be kept although coroners are free to keep all their records. However, from the nineteenth century a newspaper report is more likely to be the only surviving account.'

This certainly does not promote a robust commitment to the National Suicide Prevention Strategy (NSPS) which encourages interaction with 'concerned individuals' and is confusing as to just how coroners are 'protecting society.' While it is reasonable not to sensationalise or advertise a notorious area it is important to be transparent and present the facts. The new Coroners and Justice Bill was formally introduced in Parliament in early 2009 and received Royal Assent on 12th November 2009.
www.justice.gov.uk/news/newsrelease270308a.htm

Clifftop recovery. © H.M. Coastguards

Simple cross. © K. J. Varney

Memorials. © K. J. Varney

CHAPTER 17

Suicide Statistics

In 2007 coroners' verdicts returned by jurisdiction were in total:

259 Homicides
3007 Suicides
In East Sussex:
3 Homicides
43 Suicide
21 Open verdicts
55 Accident/misadventure

With 27 suicides at the foot of Beachy Head for 2007 (omitting open verdict, accident and misadventure)

62.8% of all suicides verdicts, returned for the whole of East Sussex, were in fact at Beachy Head.

If this many deaths occurred on a stretch of road serious action would be taken.

In 2003 the total number of deaths from around the coastline recorded by the Maritime and Coastguard Agency (MCGA) was 316. Of that total a staggering 37.3% (118) were suspected suicides, and a further 36.7% (116) were declared 'cause of death - unknown'. In the 2005 UK Annual Report, with regards to the number of deaths in the 2003/04 period, the MCGA alarmingly states: 'Regrettably, the total number of deaths is up on last year. However, the bulk of the increase is accounted for by suicide cases.' The report stated that this was an annual increase in maritime reported suicides, of 50% from the previous year. Over 29% of the total deaths were at the foot of Beachy Head.

In 2007, the MCGA released their search and rescue figures for 2006 which recorded 360 (plus 11 uncategorised) as the total number of deaths from all causes. Of that figure 105 were suicides or suspected suicides, in a year that was an all-time record low for the area of Beachy Head. Yet, if taken as a percentage, suicide equates to over a quarter of all deaths attended by the coastguards at 29.2%.

(endnote: www.mcga.gov.uk/c4mca/mcga/archives)

www.mcga.gov.uk/c4mca/mcga/archives)

When the Chaplaincy team went on patrol in 2004, it appeared that the numbers of suicides had dropped. Finally, it seemed that a positive prevention solution had been achieved. The team promptly led a local and national campaign of publicity, to highlight the low figures of suicides in 2006. This was seen as a fantastic achievement but it was to be short-lived. Month by month for 2007 and 2008 there was a steady increase, not only in the amount of incidences of suicidal and depressed people visiting the headland, as recorded by the BHCT, but in the staggering numbers of deaths.

Although it is very difficult to obtain actual numbers, detailed, year long, daily investigation has revealed the true figure of the number of people who have perished at the foot of Beachy Head. From the period between January 1st to December 31st 2007, the death toll stood, at least, at a tragic 27. These figures are identically repeated in 2008.

Most can be found in the archives of the local papers *The Brighton, Hove and Sussex Argus* and the *Eastbourne Herald* by entering keyword searches in the archives of Beachy Head: body, found, cliffs, car, depressed, suicide, jumped, plunged, leap, death, inquest and mystery. Others are recorded on the callout section of the local Royal National Lifeboat Institute's websites for Newhaven and Eastbourne. Further evidence can be found on the Sussex police website, by clicking on 'What's the helicopter doing over my house?' Others were confirmed by the Maritime Rescue Coordination Centre audits. Two more were unrecorded in the public domain for 2008 and come from local contacts, and therefore, cannot be included. Where times were reported most suicides occured between 6.11am and 12.30am with Sunday and Monday being the most common day to die. In 2008, two deaths were recorded in November and December on the BHCT website but not reported by local press and, therefore, are not included in these figures. Sunday was the most common day of death for 2008.

	Male			**Female**			**?Body found**		
	07	**08**	**09**	**07**	**08**	**09**	**07**	**08**	**09**
Mon	2	2	2	4	2	1	1	0	0
Tue	2	2	3	1	1	0	0	0	0
Wed	1	1	2	1	0	1	2	0	0
Thu	0	3	4	1	0	1	0	0	0
Fri	0	1	1	2	1	0	1	0	0
Sat	1	3	2	1	1	0	0	1	0
Sun	6	0	4	1	4	3	0	3	0
Total	**12**	**12**	**18**	**11**	**9**	**6**	**4**	**4**	**0**

It is interesting to note that more males died on a Sunday and more females chose to perish on a Monday in 2007. No males died on Thursday or Friday. March and July had no deaths but April is the commonest month for self-destruction at five. Where the term used was male and female as opposed to 'body recovered' there were 11 female deaths to 12 male using this violent method.

In 2008 no females perished on Wednesday or Thursday, Sunday appears to have no males but the gender of the bodies recovered have not been disclosed. May was by far the most common month of recorded deaths.

In 2009 no females died on Tuesday, Friday or Saturday.

Previous end year totals (excluding misadventure/accident and open verdicts) were:

2009 24	2008 27	2007 27	2006 7
2005 26	2004 34	2003 17	2002 15

BHCT have a breakdown of figures from September 2006 published on their website: www.bhct.org.uk

	Incidents	**Suicidal**	**Death**
2006			
August	29		
September	51	12	
October	46	12	
November	38	8	
December	38	18	
2007			
January	59	17	
February	35	9	
March	45	13	
(New Chaplain appointed: introducing an increase to 100 hours of patrols per week)			
April	67	20	4
May	67	28	
June	59	32	
July	54	25	
August	67	21	
September	49	18	2
October	77	35	
November	45	16	
December	46	14	
Total	**670**	**248**	**6**

Figures for the year were announced on their website (12/09/07) August 2006

- July 2007 as 588 incidents, 205 were suicidal + 10 'other persons'.

On 2nd January 2008 the BHCT summarised their work for the whole of 2007:

'During 2007 BHCT were involved in 670 incidents/searches for those in distress resulting in the rescue of 248 persons who were depressed or suicidal. These figures show an increase of 211 incidents with 114 persons rescued, over the figures of 2006.' There is no total for the number of deaths.

The toll for 2008 also makes grim reading.

2008	**Incidents**	**Suicidal**	**Deaths**
January	46	17	1
February	50	19	1
March	70	19	2
April	69	26	2
May	78	27	6
June	62	17	2
July	66	16	2
August	54	11	2
September	41	11	3
October	59	23	1
November	55	12	2
December	49	19	2
Total	**699**	**217**	**26**
2009			
January	46	14	1
February	41	12	1
March	55	15	2
April	47	15	1
May	59	14	5
June	115	50	2
July	90	42	NR
August	74	26	1
September	59	34	3
October	74	34	2
November	71	20	NR
December	51	21	NR

The chaplaincy team now runs a fleet of red vehicles. Gone are the knitted jumpers with large black crucifixes on the front. They are easily spotted in their new highly visible pillar box-red uniforms and have increased their patrol hours to 100 a week, supported by a 24-hour on-call team. The number of volunteers has fluctuated from 16 to 22 members from 14 different churches, with three full-time ministers employed. According to their summer 2007 newsletter, BHCT state: 'In the 9-month period up to the end of April 2007 we have been involved in 410 incidents and searches. From those searches we have been involved in directly finding and helping 120 people at Beachy Head who were depressed or suicidal. If this trend continues we expect to be dealing with 500 incidents and around 160 persons in our third year. (Aug 2006 - July 2007).'

In 2009 they recorded 782 incidents/searches, an increase of 11%, and 283 rescues of suicidal people, an increase of 30%.

Why are the figures increasing? Surely they should be diminishing.

It may be argued that an increase in patrols has led to the unprecedented upsurge in the amount of incidents. The ethos of the team is to be 'a deterrent to those who are considering coming to Beachy Head to end their lives'. But without the previous extra intervention were these sorrowful souls simply visiting the cliffs and then returning back to the isolation of their existence? Where in society are they placed when they are rescued from the brink of God's gateway?

The BHCT, for all its good intentions, have no association with local authorities except a close working relationship with the coastguards. They are not trained, advised or associated with any mental health associations such as the Samaritans, Sane, or Mind, and have no means to track the welfare of those who are returned to social care. They may also be attracting attention seekers or the homeless and disaffected people rejected by the National Health Service as 'nuisance regulars.' In September 2008 Pastor Ross Hardy left the BHCT to continue his calling with the More Fire Revival Ministries www.morefire.org.uk. The new team leader elected was Clair McGinty-Gibbs who on Sunday 25th June 2006 was woken by the 'precious Holy Spirit'. She suddenly felt she needed to find a church so she gathered up her family and went to Pevensey Bay where luck would have it the Baptist church was having a beach service. The Pastor was conducting a sermon on new beginnings as he baptized people in the sea. Clair suddenly declared her new commitment to Christ and ran into the sea to be baptised. She claims the Lord spoke to her and her husband about a role on the headland as a chaplain. In September 2008 she took up her new role. It is difficult to fully understand whether they are the right organisation to be wandering the Downs in search of those who come to Beachy Head at their most forlorn. At the end of August 2009 she left the team and Ross Hardy returned to carry on his commitment to salvation.

Since 2005 the BHCT have made a conscious decision not to attract media attention to their presence on the cliffs: 'We as a charity then chose to refuse all enquiries by the media for articles and interviews.' However they do make selective announcements. Despite any qualms, their integrity and commitment is unflinching and they were awarded the Spring Harvest Innovation Award in 2006 by Faithworks for their dedication.

Globally, there are, according to the World Health Organisation (WHO), one million suicides a year. That is 16 per 100,000 per population or one every 40 seconds. In 2006, there were 229,601 recorded deaths in England and Wales of which inquests were carried out on 29,327. With one suicide every 88 minutes and suicide being the biggest cause of death among males under the age of 35, in England and Wales, it is surprising to view the statistics. The highest rates are usually recorded as accident or misadventure which makes it impossible to prove the number of actual suicides, either nationally or at Beachy Head, although it is safe to say that the official statistics still do not reflect the number of deaths, as opposed to suicide, at this hotspot.

The decisions of coroners reflect a reluctance to review the criteria for recording a verdict of suicide, even when there is evidence to suggest that up to 40% of those who commit suicide have attempted it previously. endnote: eds Hawton K and Heeringen K van (First pub 2000) *The International Handbook of Suicide and Attempted Suicide* John Wiley & Sons Chichester).

A suicide note is considered the only defining proof of intention, but such messages are only left by 30% of cases and even less are found at Beachy Head. The burden of proof falls on circumstantial evidence and the vagaries of the coroner. This was the extraordinary case as reported in the *Brighton, Hove and Sussex Evening Argus* (25/7/75) when a 21-year-old man travelled from Yorkshire with a friend intent on killing himself. He was already receiving help for his suicidal behaviour. Previously, he had thrown himself out of a window but had only sustained minor injuries. The next day he severely slashed his wrists and was rushed to hospital for a blood transfusion.

The day after he was signed out of hospital he tried to throw himself off a roof but friends managed to stop him. All his attempts so far had been futile. His friends intervened again the same day when he tried to take a deadly cocktail of drugs and alcohol. Another friend who, perhaps, wasn't aware of his suicidal tendencies agreed to travel with him on a summer's day to Beachy Head. There the young man chose the most lethal and non-refundable method to die.

Arriving at the cliff top he suddenly ran towards the cliff edge, his friend desperately reached out, grabbing for his coat. It is recorded that the man told his last saviour: 'If you don't let go I will take you with me'. His friend had no choice, as he struggled to get free, terrifyingly close to the crumbling edge; he had to let him go for the final time. His death was pronounced as an 'open verdict'. According to the coroner, Alan Craze, the man had never clearly stated his suicidal intentions.

Coroners' verdicts for England and Wales, 2006

	Male	Female
• Industrial disease	12%	2%
• Natural causes	23%	28%
• Drug related	3%	1%
• Suicide	13%	9%
• Open verdict	9%	8%
• Accident or misadventure	31%	40%
• All other	9%	12%

Results, as published by Department for Constitutional Affairs, Statistics on Coroners Bulletins 2006. (endnote: Statistical Bulletin 2006 www.dca.gov.uk/statistics/coroners.htm)

Is the National Suicide Prevention Strategy working?

Official statistics are not recorded in a consistent format and are often difficult to access. Compared to coroners' findings in 2006, the format makes it difficult to carry out a robust interrogation. In contrast, the NSPS statistics are recorded as:

	Male	Female
• Hanging/strangling/suffocation	50%	31%
• Drug related/poisoning	19%	40%
• Motor gas poisoning	6%	2%
• Drowning	4%	7%
• Jumping/falling before a moving object	4%	3%
• Jumping/falling from high place	3%	5%
• Sharp object	3%	1%
• Firearms/explosives	3%	0.5%
• Smoke/fire/gas fumes	2%	2%
• Other	7%	8%

How can any conclusions be extracted or compared from such diverse and manipulated data that is so inconsistent in the reporting method? The Office for National Statistics (ONS) has updated its website with 'Corrected Suicide Rates' in the UK, from 1991 to 2004. This uses a ranking system by area to highlight the places that have the highest incidence of suicide. If you just look at these corrected figures alone female suicides in Eastbourne are ranked at 24. But if you then look at the figures for England and Wales over the years 2000 to 2003, Eastbourne overall ranks at number seven with 19 suicides per 100,000 population and both male and female rates now move up to joint fifth.

The South Coast of England, and in particular Eastbourne, needs special attention as the overall figure at 19 per 100,000 population is significantly above the global mortality rate of 16 per 100,000. Part of the remit of the NSPS is that local delivery plans are supposed to be published and scrutinised yearly (2005-2008) but when contacted, the East Sussex figures were not available on the Primary Care Trust (PCT) website and the East Sussex Suicide Prevention Strategy report does not publish audited figures. When contacted the PCT was unable to retrieve any audit figures, as the responsibility for mental health issues has been given to the Sussex Partnership NHS Trust which is spread over three districts and does not have a central computer network. Eventually, the Audit and Effectiveness Manager for Mental Health and Social Care, was able to offer access to 'Draft 3 (8 October 2004) East Sussex Suicide Prevention Strategy 2004-2009'.

This was the latest available report (as opposed to a yearly audit) and once again stated contradictory evidence. The author and Chair, Dr Jennifer Bennett, notes on page 29: 'During the foot and mouth outbreak Beachy Head was closed and inaccessible. There were no suicides there during that year.' On page 31, quoting an extract from a research project by Dr Isaac Mokhtar, entitled *Suicide by Jumping: Gender difference and Impact of Accessibility 1987-2001*, the conflicting quote states, 'It is interesting to note that in the year 2001 (Foot and Mouth Crisis) Beachy Head was not accessible by car and there was no single suicide until it re-opened in June 2001, there then followed 6 cases of male suicide and 3 cases of female suicide for the rest of the year.'

So where do the ONS get their statistics? Coroners, even under the new reform bill, drawn up, following the Harold Shipman enquiry, are not obliged to reveal their verdicts.

In contrast, statistics from the coroner's office that covers the Golden Gate Bridge, in a ten year report, found that over 85% of deaths were by residents within the Bay area, compared to 32% for the Eastbourne area. Local audits will never be able to capture true figures for deaths at this sorrowful place on the south coast of England or come any closer to finding an effective prevention strategy unless there is co-operation across all government service providers to find a no-blame, face the facts, intelligent debate on policy to target 'hotspots' and introduce specific responsibility, local research and effective prevention.

Other factors that confuse detailed research are that information is not recorded on a yearly basis, locally, or at the ONS, and records for England mostly include figures from Wales. But this government policy (NSPS) is directed at England only so how will results in 2010 be measured or compared? The view that society is judged in the global world economically, socially and spirituality by, amongst other things, its suicide rate, seems to reflect a less-than-robust attitude to transparent recording of the number of people dying by their own hand. ('Misadventure' and 'accident' do not feature in any of the statistics although 'open verdict' does).

It will be interesting to see if the new independent Statistics Board that came into effect in April 2008 has enough teeth to really tackle the recording of official figures. Their formation came after the Statistics and Registration Act received Royal Assent in July 2007. The aim is to: 'Promote and safeguard the production and publication of official statistics that serve the public good; and the quality, good practice and comprehensiveness of official statistics.' (endnote: Independence for National Statistics.
www.statistics.gov.uk/about/data/independence/default.asp)

Lighthouse view. © K. J. Varney

Four different remembrance tokens. © K. J. Varney

Beachy Head lighthouse. © K. J. Varney

Chapter 18

Suicide Prevention

All the world's leading suicide hotspots are, in fact, jumping sites. With this in mind, a policy was published to focus on proactive measures, to reduce suicide and attempted suicide from jumping. This policy, dated 2002, clearly states as part of the objectives an aim to: 'Reduce the number of suicides as a result of jumping from high places.' Under 'Goal 3 Action Under Way' it offers a principle: 'The Samaritans have posted contact numbers on a number of bridges and other high places.'

The Samaritans dedicated sign at Beachy Head has, in fact, been in place since 1976. It is positioned next to the phone box at the cliff peak, offering would-be jumpers a last resort contact, a silent hand to hold, one final stay of execution. But the bus from Eastbourne stops 100 ft away from it on the side of the cliffs. Approaching from Birling Gap, to the west, the sign has its back to you. The Samaritans had no recorded evidence of its effectiveness. Then in March 2010 a new sign was generously funded by the Hailsham Lions Club. The sign is improved with a reflective notice and the Samaritans phone number is now on all the car park machines, yet it is still in the same position as before.

So, at the leading hotspot in the world, only one new active prevention method has been introduced. No audit or monitoring tools have been implemented and the Samaritans continue their tireless work that, for the past 34 years, has been simply to erect a sign and hope for the best. In June 2007 the press office of the Samaritans confirmed in good faith that: 'There are a number of sites around the country that are known as "suicide hotspots". However, no 'map' of these exists within the Department of Health (DoH) or any voluntary sector agency. We are probably ideally placed to do this (since our 202 branches will almost certainly know where their local hotspots are) but we lack the resources to undertake such an exercise.'

The Eastbourne branch stated that they 'have no specific figures how many people call us from that location', but were able to provide general figures for 2006 as:

Telephone contacts 13,838
Face to face contacts 565
Answered e-mails 902

Cliff edge. © K. J. Varney

This is below the average of 25,279 total contacts per branch. Despite the fact that the Samaritans have never researched the effectiveness of this sign the Bridgend, Wales branch appealed to the Vale of Glamorgan council to erect a similar sign at Southerndown Cliffs near Ogmore, the scene of nine suicides in three years. The cliffs are owned by Dunraven Estates who support the Samaritans in their proposal, a spokeswoman commenting to the BBC News in 2003 said: 'When the Samaritans approached us, I was a bit sceptical at first but they have said that it has been proven to work at Beachy Head.' (endnote: BBC News Help signs plan at suicide cliffs. http://www.news.bbc.co.uk/archives)

In January 2008 the Samaritans issued an article on their website called 'Tackling Suicide in 2008'. It shows a photo of a number of officials and volunteers standing beside a small white sign attached to a supporting balustrade on the Tyne Bridge. The sign carries details of the Samaritans telephone contact number in a bid to encourage would-be jumpers to call them before they take the deadly plunge. The text in the report is encouraging in tone: 'No single agency is responsible for suicide prevention and there is strong evidence-based research which shows that signs encourage people with suicidal feelings to seek help. Signs featuring Samaritans' telephone number are already in place at a number of well-known locations e.g. the Clifton Suspension Bridge, Beachy Head & the cliff tops at Roker.' Now would-be jumpers, accessing the website, have other alternative 'hotspots' to choose from, and the evidence-based research is not referenced.

There is no denying that the Samaritans do offer a highly regarded, global service that is like a valued friend to vulnerable, despairing people but have they got it right at Beachy Head? From warm busy offices it must be difficult to imagine that well-thought-out strategies, implemented then ignored for over 30 years, are as useful to anyone standing at the cliff edge, as the passing clouds. Yet of the 5.2 million people a year who call the Samaritans only 21% were suicidal in 2007. So if 90 % of people who chose suicide at Beachy Head

rates are unavailable. This figure is again sadly changing. In 2007 there were at least 27 deaths between the cliffs at Beachy Head and Peacehaven, including Birling Gap, the original site of the coastguard huts and cottages. 2008 saw another 27 tragic deaths and 2009 24 deaths.

According to lifeboat crews, Birling Gap and Seaford, further west of the lighthouse, are becoming more popular places to jump due to the high visual presence of the Chaplaincy team that patrol on the most notorious spots on the headland. Those determined to jump do not want to be prevented or preached to. Prevention and intervention are subjects that are under constant scrutiny. The cliffs at Beachy Head present a unique problem. Fencing off the area would certainly detract from its attraction as a place of outstanding beauty and would need to be replaced frequently due to the erratic erosion of the landscape.

The prevention strategy 'Action to be Taken' aimed to develop guidance on suicide hotspots from high places but does not focus on actual deaths. Since it was implemented in 2002 little seems to have changed. Statistics vary for numerous reasons. It is hard to give conclusions because one set of data is an unmatched jigsaw piece to others. In the (undated) report 'Guidance of Action to be taken at Suicides Hotspots' the positive conclusions are that overall the figures are relatively low: 'In 2004 there were 154 cases of suicide by jumping in England and Wales accounting for 3% of all suicides and open verdicts' which, if matched with figures from Beachy Head for that year, means that 22% of this national total (34) were recorded suicides (excluding accidents/open verdicts/misadventure) at the foot of the cliffs. The actual percentage is probably far greater.

Undeniably, urgent attention must be given to this place with a focused, local research strategy that breaks the boundaries of taboo, media silence and hushed up figures. As noted by Al Alvarez: 'Only one generalization is wholly certain and generally agreed: that statistics reflect at best only a fraction of the real figures, which various authorities reckon to be anything between a quarter and half as large again.'

The NSPS forum was given all this data, with full evidence, to be discussed and acted on in November 2007. Although fully supportive of the research it seems the initial task was to contact the local coroner's office to verify the death figures. By March 2009 no information had been retrieved. However, a forum is now in discussion with the consultant in Public Health for East Sussex to try and find prevention methods other than media silence to help this beautiful, troubled place. Ideas put forward from this research include: a review of current signage, a telephone alert sign with a phone number directly connected to the local coastguards which will significantly reduce response

Sign. © *K. J. Varney*

times, a place of safety on the cliff top where anyone who is feeling suicidal can be taken and offered immediate counselling, a psychological barrier along the cliff edge, an association with local mental health groups, guidance to support the Beachy Head Chaplaincy Team, a memorial / contemplation garden. Prevention is key but as difficult as knowing the colour of the wind. For the sake of all that follow this sad path in years to come and the brave men and women who descend the cliffs to recover them I hope the wind is yellow.

If you or someone close to you is feeling suicidal ask for help now.

Samaritans 24 hour help line 08457 90 90 90 www.samaritans.org

CHAPTER 19

The Journey

The fateful fall is usually no accident. Every route to Beachy Head is a bleak journey of both body and mind. Every turn of the wheel, every roll of the train, and every sorrowful footstep detaches it from being an impulsive act.

It takes an arduous three-mile trek on foot from Eastbourne rail station, through the bustling town centre, to get to the base of the long climb, and onwards. Alternatively, catching the red and yellow tourist buses, with their sliced roofs, carries a bleak, ironic message: 'Hop On Hop Off' is blazoned on the rear advertising as it winds its way back to town. Alighting from the bus there are only two definitive options: to attempt to die or be forever captivated by a mesmerizing landscape.

For just a few pounds, a taxi driver will take you, no questions asked. Local cab drivers openly admit that those people that request Beachy Head as their destination cause them to tilt the interior mirror and carefully watch the faces of their passengers. They are looking for typical clues: red-rimmed eyes, shabby demeanor, absence of camera, rucksack or tourist trappings. With a practised

Original Beachy Head hotel. *By permission of the Countryside Centre*

eye, they are able to spot a potential suicide victim, and with experienced cunning, signal on their radio a coded message, to be passed to Sussex police that a jumper may be on board.

'Hop on hop off' bus. © K. J. Varney

Once up there, at the side of the road, there is a large sign with contact details for the Samaritans, but it sits in black and white obscurity next to the ice cream van in his usual spot in the left-hand corner of the car park. From his little box of glacial pleasure he also watches in silence. All places where someone may just spot that your patent loneliness is solitary and try to barge in.

At Beachy Head, at least five suicides a week are averted by the vigilance of local people. The Countryside Centre and visitor's car park are just 100m from the deadly cliff edge. Next to the car park is the Beachy Head pub, locally referred to as the 'Last Stop'. Staff are trained to spot potential victims by their behaviour. These warnings include weeping, excessive drinking,

Beachy Head pub. © K. J. Varney

erratic or incomprehensible conversation or an open declaration of their intention. In 2007, the local town of Hailsham began an initiative in 38 of its pubs to train staff to approach drinkers who displayed potential suicidal tendencies. This was met with some reluctance by the publicans. One landlady is quoted as saying: 'Will staff be qualified enough to make a judgement on such a thing? I wouldn't want to make a judgement on someone and I'm the house manager.'

Over 90% of deaths at the cliffs are thought to be by people with either known psychiatric problems or others who have suffered a recent emotional upset. Licensing staff alert the local police to attend to a potential incident but are forbidden by their employers from discussing events with customers. On some occasions they have physically restrained suspect jumpers for their own safety.

Ice cream man. © K. J. Varney

None of us know what it is really like to die. Everyone has suffered a loss, stood by a graveside, seen the true waste of the light of the departed, then lit a candle to guide their path. Should those who choose their time and place be treated differently? Al Alvarez writes, having been brought back from the brink one Christmas, following an overdose: 'I assume now that death, when it finally comes, will probably be nastier than suicide, and certainly a great deal less convenient.' (endnote: Alvarez A *The Savage God* London 1971).

Suicide is often seen as an impulsive act, fuelled by drugs, alcohol or spurned love. But the journey to Beachy Head offers plenty of time for reflection, meditations and doubt. It is almost impossible to think what might have been going through the mind of terminally ill, 65-year-old, Terry Windsor. On Tuesday 6th May 2008, Terry Windsor, loaded his Renault Laguna with two bottles of oxygen, just enough to maintain his failing, cancer-ridden lungs for one final journey. Leaving his home at the Rushey Hill caravan park in Peacehaven, he drove to Beachy Head. At around 5.45pm, just half an hour after his family had reported him missing, a local police community support officer spotted a car 150 ft down the cliffs. A man matching Mr Windsor's description was found dead in the driver's seat. His family, later, had the sad task of formally identifying his body.

On Saturday 27th February 2010 the sun made a welcome glow on the headland after a harsh, bitter winter. The coastguards made an early start to retrieve the body of a woman from Kent. Her car had been found in a lay-by the previous evening, the door left open as if she had rushed from it, running the final100m to hurl herself from the cliffs. The rescue team walked the shore to where she lay but couldn't reach her so called in the RNLI inshore lifeboat. They too were unable to get to her remains. By this time the Sussex police helicopter had arrived as support and as they hovered to land they spotted another body of a woman from London. Eventually as a joint effort both bodies were taken to the local hospital. But as the helicopter began its return journey just a few miles along the coast they spotted a third body. This time it was a young man just 21 who had been missing from his home in Hampshire.

In 1997, David Gunnell, a leading authority on suicide by jumping, published a review article which noted that more than 50% of those who jump from Beachy Head come from outside East Sussex. Thirteen years on that figure, according to the *East Sussex Healthcare Trust Action Plan 2006*, is now 68%. So, considering that just 32% of deaths at the foot of the cliffs are by local residents, many must leave home as usual setting off in their car. From London the journey to Beachy Head takes, on a good day about one and a half hours. What could that really be like? A fictional tale to most; a deadly journey for others.

Imagine driving away from London with all its pressure way behind you as you turn onto the A23 Brighton road on a sunny, crisp November morning. The sun has barely kissed the sky and the first dawn birds are waking. Just above eye level ahead, the South Downs are shrouded in a blue hue of mist and fog, rising magnificently above the newly-laid tarmac. The road ahead, for now, is clear. Farmhouses dot the landscape with smoke quaintly billowing from age-old chimneys. The first flights have begun to leave Heathrow airport criss-crossing the sky. Cold engines rumble and groan as they merge into the traffic lanes on their rat run to work.

As a sleepy-eyed voyeur of the landscape you take a moment to enjoy the autumn leaves still clinging to the wintry trees, softly purple and gold, barely a breeze to shake them from their branches. Then the phone rings, shrilling into the space; still aware of the rules, your thumb automatically finds the red button and switches it off before throwing it onto the empty passenger seat. More cars now enter the main road, squeezing into the line of traffic, switching to the outside lane to get a speed up. They pass your car totally unaware of where you are headed or why.

Your mood changes, swaying with each turn of the wheel from excited anticipation to fear to quiet resignation. The radio DJ is irritating in his Monday morning cheerfulness but the traffic report cuts in with warnings of delays,

Eastbourne pier. © K. J. Varney

roadworks just up ahead, slowing the fatal progress and anger rises. Questions swirl around your head, interrupting best-laid plans; the world is stirring to life: too many people, too many cars. What if something goes wrong? This isn't the first time you have made this journey. Last time, you made a dry run to get the landscape fixed in your head, and prepare the route to the finest detail. So you wouldn't get caught. Finally, the traffic flow resumes; you notice an old Escort ahead and can't help but smile then sigh. Memories evoked of another life so far away, gone forever.

On the road goes, you wave a 'thank you' to the car behind as it lets you ease into the correct lane on the A22 towards Eastbourne, but they don't wave back; grim-faced they begrudge the six ft they've allowed you, if only they knew that soon a six foot space was indeed waiting for you. Just four miles left to go. On the side of the road a big, smiley sign 'The Sunshine Coast' welcomes you. There is still time to turn around, and, suddenly, panic forces a flash of doubt: put it off, try again tomorrow like giving up smoking, always an excuse. Why not? Then the chalk white hills come into view at last, dazzling white, whiter than last time like giant, friendly white smiling teeth topped with the shorn grass, gracefully chewed by the ever-present sheep. And the brown tourist sign to Beachy Head gives a little wink. Passing Treasure Island, a childish fantasy playground of yesterday's hopes, mocking the mood now; inanimate objects strangely morphing as the watchers of your soul. From the corner of the world, the Channel enters the scene for the first time, the rising sun reflecting shafts of glittering gold on its pale surface. The Victorian

Eastbourne pier stands splendidly on elegant cast-iron legs, wading in the surf.

Suddenly the urban landscape takes over, and hotel after hotel rushes by. Immaculate carpet gardens fringe the promenade and retired folk occupy breakfast rooms and benches, barely making it across pedestrian crossings before the red turns to green. The Wish Tower evokes nothing, no meaning is attached to its name, like the emptiness of a wishing well throwing your dreams and desires into the darkness. Now it's real, really real as the road begins to climb, cutting a scar through the Downs, the sun eclipsed in the shadow of the hawthorn trees. Just ahead now is the highest point of the cliffs. Pulling the car to a halt there are three decisions to make: park the car, and walk the 100m to the cliff edge; rev the car's engine and charge over the cliff; or turn around and go home.

You sit, so quietly. There are no animals or birds or insects, no sound of the sea or the wind or your tears. Another car pulls in, another lone driver. There's still time to change your mind; barely any cars have followed from the town, so you watch them, locking the car, walking away, not even glancing your way. No 'good morning' smile, or nod of the head. You already no longer exist. The phone is silent on the seat beside you. You pick it up. It's time to send a final message. Is that it? Not romantic, heroic, or worth it, a vital life now a bleak statistic, another family left in wretched mourning. There is no need to fill this despair with more pain. Walk away, find someone to talk to, give life another chance at least for today. One day at a time.

Maybe walking to the edge will be different; maybe someone will notice a sorrowful heart.

It certainly wasn't the case for one 30-year-old man, when he left his home one day resigned to jumping from the Golden Gate Bridge. After his body had been retrieved from the Bay the medical examiner went to visit his home, dreading breaking the terrible news to his family. When he arrived, nobody was there to answer the door; when he eventually got inside the apartment, he found bare, dismal rooms showing all the signs of a man living alone. On the man's bureau was a handwritten note. As he recalls the incident 30 years on, he claims he has never forgotten what the note read: 'I'm going to walk to the bridge. If one person smiles at me on the way, I will not jump.'

Surprisingly, some people survive the fall and live to tell the tale. This was the case of another man who went to the Golden Gate Bridge to die. Kevin Hines was just 18 years old when he boarded a bus in 2000. He recalls treating himself to what was to be his last meal: a feast of Starbursts and Skittles, before heading out to the walkway. Once there, he began fearfully pacing backwards and forwards. He spent half an hour sobbing without one single person asking him if he was okay. Then he remembers a beautiful German tourist tapping him on the shoulder; as he turned to her she held out a camera and asked him in broken English if he would take a photo for her - which he did. Then he climbed over the gangway: 'I was like, Fuck this, nobody cares. So I jumped.' (endnote: *The New Yorker* Jumpers 2003)

Making that final decision may be far from impulsive. By returning to the same plot, planning each move, rehearsing the final act is like stalking death, in the same way obsessive people stalk the living; those in most despair stalk their own lives. Creating deep in their being a total fearlessness for when the trigger is pulled, self-preservation fleeing, the self-murder is done. In that moment no one is hurt, the burden is lifted.

Al Alvarez is sceptical of the whole idea that anyone simply makes a decision to die. He calls suicide a tormentor that re-visits your conscience, haunting everyday life. Perhaps his notion is that you can wake from your dreams but never your nightmares. To truly know if the act was an impulsive one is only known by those who survive, yet they seem to reject their misery, suddenly embarrassed: 'They can return to life, that is, only by denying the strength of their despair, transforming their unconscious but deliberate choice into an impulsive, meaningless mistake. They wanted to die without seeming to mean it.'(endnote: 1971 Alvarez A *The Savage God* London Weidenfeld and Nicholson)

Thomas Joiner, clinical psychologist, also examines this, pushing forward a theory that the powerful, lethal will to overcome the natural instinct of self-preservation, must stem from a desire to practise self-harm. The 'cry for help' theory really does have a place in catastrophic events that lead to the final act: 40% of suicides have a history of self-harm. Yet the 'cry for help' term carries the stigma of failure for the person and is viewed by others as a form of attention-seeking.

If Thomas Joiner is right in his theory which he claims 'has been neglected by theorists and researchers'; maybe the reasons behind suicide can finally be tackled. He questions why many people who tolerate immense suffering in life never go on to kill themselves while others choose to end their lives:

'It may be that few people want to die by suicide, but also, and perhaps more important, that even fewer can. Self-injury, especially when severe, has the potential to be painful and fear-inducing. Who can tolerate such high levels of pain, fear and the like? The view taken here is that those who have gotten used to the negative aspects of suicide, and additionally, who have acquired competence and even courage specifically regarding suicide, are the only ones capable of the act - anyone else is unable to complete suicide, even if they want to.'

With each attempt at self-harm the method and severity become more lethal. The fear diminishes with each practice enabling mental rehearsals towards a violent end. An example of this fearfulness is illustrated by the life and death of musician, Kurt Cobain:

'Cobain was temperamentally fearful - afraid of needles, afraid of heights, and afraid of guns. Through repeated exposure and practice, a person initially afraid of needles, heights and guns later became a daily self-injecting drug user, someone who climbed and dangled from thirty-foot scaffolding during concerts (at which times, incidentally, he would yell, "I'm going to kill myself!"), and someone who enjoyed shooting guns. Regarding guns, Cobain initially felt that they were barbaric and wanted nothing to do with them; later he agreed to go with his friend to shoot guns but would not get out of the car; on later excursions, he got out of the car but would not touch the guns; and on still later trips, he agreed to let his friend show him how to aim and fire. Cobain died by a self-inflicted gunshot wound in 1994 at the age of twenty seven.' (endnote: 2005 Joiner T *Why people die by suicide* Harvard College USA).

There are also the masquerading deaths of the slow suicide. Everyone has had contact with the wilful destructive nature of alcoholics, anorexics, drug addicts, smokers, self-harmers, even the adrenalin junkies who all dance with death. They are all dicing with destiny but their intentions have crept under the radar, keeping the violent self-sacrifice of a suicide as the only abhorrent act of them all. But jumping from a cliff or bridge is a result of years of learned behaviour that is still treated in society as an act of impulsive insanity.

Dr Lanny Berman, executive director of the American Association of Suicidology, believes: 'Suicidal people have transformation fantasies and are prone to magical thinking, like children and psychotics.' Thomas Joiner also believes that the suicidal practice the final act, mentally, as well as physically: playing and replaying a vivid, intense and long-lasting ideation; a picture-perfect scene in their mind's eye of their death. This type of mental and physical rehearsal increases the tragic potential to carry it through.

Real men and women, friends, lovers, daughters, fathers, not just statistics, all choosing the long solemn journey to one solitary place; a place where life flourishes on a splendid canvas of nature, a solemn voyage to a public self-execution granting yourself a last request, a favourite meal, a touching goodbye, a cigarette, a lover's kiss, a mother's smile. Who knows at what stage the decision is made? These are all just words: romantic, fatalistic, voyeur-of-terror expressions. In reality, standing at that precipice of peace maybe chaos has ascended, fleeing from the consciousness: the calamity of life's voyage no longer challenging, and the decision to take your own life a distant memory; only the inevitable is left.

This doesn't need to be your journey. There is always time to walk away, ask for help and survive to live another day.

For most people the whole idea of jumping from a high cliff is a terrifying thought; even if it is a spur-of-the-moment decision, you would imagine the fear would save you, and pull you back. So it's the 'how' as well as the eternal question of 'why': how does anyone actually go through with it? Does time become suspended during those final seven seconds? Ann McGuire having survived the four-second fall from the Golden Gate Bridge in 1979 remembers thinking on the way down: 'I must be about to hit, three times!' Dr Keith Ramesar, Consultant pathologist, Eastbourne District General Hospital, claims: 'There is no reason at all for anyone going unconscious as they are falling from the cliffs at Beachy Head. I believe they are still aware of what's happening all the way down until the ground rush.'

Spiritualists think differently. They believe that the consciousness is multi-dimensional; the conscious mind indeed slows everything down as it awaits the outcome of a traumatic event, but as the higher levels of consciousness become aware, through space and time, that the body will not survive, it jumps or flees:

The consciousness realising its fate will be looking down waiting to know what will happen next, the life force will remain with the body until it can no longer support that life any longer. Once the life force and the consciousness have departed from the body they reform together on what is known as the mid-plain of existence as the etheric body. From here the essence of that person's soul will be commanded by Universal laws. Those that have been suffering trauma of the heart or soul in life will wander the mid-plain as what are called ghosts, until they are guided, through projecting love and healing, to the spiritual realm.

If you listen to the breeze it is said that you will hear the sirens of Greek mythology who tried to lure Ulysses and his sailors to destruction. The Falling Sands sends shivers of chalk to the beach below Beachy Head, echoing a silence. So what really happens at this windswept, mystical, tragic, spellbinding place? The cliffs of desolation remain hidden from the undisturbed, simply chanced upon on a local seaside visit.

The mournful, the hopeless, the damned, know exactly how to find it. Technology has entered their lives, pin numbers to get in with no codes to get out, blunt knives to scar the body, letting the energy out with light momentary relief. Not a perceived cry for help, but a real flood of pain, old-fashioned blood-letting. The parallel world that surrounds depression or severe emotional loss still functions trance-like; needs barely met, simply following the rules of social acceptance; a phone that never rings. E-mails full of junk, a

Path up to the Downs. © K. J. Varney

perceived life with no value, time lost, circling the hours until the circle breaks. A satellite blinks above, bright as the north Star, carrying the final text message on the dark horizon.

The lighthouse toiling a nightshift seeks out lost souls of the ocean but like society with its back half-turned, it doesn't shine its light on the most needy and the lighthouse will soon suffer the same useless fate; pretty to look at, but with no real function. Set adrift to preserve itself with no means to do so, floating in a sea of uncertainty. In the dawn of the 21st century for all its liberations, expectations, preventions, interceptions, and promise, was less than enchanting for Joss, Jonathan, Sarah, Damon, Christine and Jonathan, Hinah, Ross, Melanie, Giles, Renaud, Susan, body, remains and all the others archived, still, to the north of the earth, far from the east of eternal promise and hope. Not even the eternal rest of a true statistic.

Path from Cow Gap. © K. J. Varney

While this place is known as the valley of the damned, the magnetism will continue to draw the most disheartened to prove that finally they believe they can do something right. The lighthouse is now empty, but the lantern still guards the sea. On the headland the new keepers of the light are those dedicated teams of volunteers who spend their own precious time trying to save lives. Keith Lane with his once-daily patrols, the Chaplaincy Team, the lifeboat crews, the coastguards, and the Eastbourne and Birling Gap Cliff Rescue Teams are all the real lights in the darkness. Their dedication, bravery and compassion driven by a mission to save the lives of people who come to this beautiful place to die.

Chapter 20

The Final Taboo

In a modern society it is hard to comprehend that suicide is still the 'gravest taboo', ranking above murder, paedophilia, mass murder and genocide. Despite the silence around the subject, especially at Beachy Head, each and every day the media report news about threats of, or attempted suicide. The actions of suicide bombers have entered into mainstream reporting, as well as celebrity gossip, spreading news about human frailty: Amy Winehouse, Chris Langham, George Michael, Stephen Fry, Kerry Katona, Paris Hilton, Nicole Ritchie, Britney Spears, Whitney Houston, Michael Barrymore, Robbie Williams . . . all of them have hit the headlines at some stage or another for their mental health issues.

Yet, in every day life, there is a conspiracy of silence. Everyone knows that suicide happens but nobody wants to talk about it. The media have been instructed to be wary when reporting what is called 'completed suicide'. Journalists are taught to take a sensitive approach, and dramas have to portray a positive outcome just in case it creates a 'copycat' effect. The Samaritans acknowledge that there is a dilemma. They see it as a valid subject, that the media has a role to play in educating the public about suicide, and offers detailed guidelines to the media. But 'completed suicide' evokes a deep insecurity, a fear that if it is discussed honestly it will somehow infect society, and cause a contagion where blame will fall at the feet of those who dare speak about it.

Eric Steel, having filmed a year of activity at the Golden Gate Bridge confirms the hushed attitude to suicide: 'In the United States there are almost twice as many suicides each year than homicides. While homicides are a nightly recitation on the local news, suicides are rarely mentioned.'

Why is there still such a terrible shame attached to suicide? Perhaps it forces people to think about their own capability to choose death over life; terror deeply embedded in the human psyche that suicide is still a mortal sin that will be judged at inquest, in a court of law and displayed as a weakness over strength. Dying to be loved when self-love has escaped.

The mere mention of suicide in the 21st century still resonates with the dark corners of the past. Like the mad auntie locked in the attic it is an unspoken anguish never to be truly explored and, thereby, understood. The door is firmly closed on the million people, worldwide, who commit suicide every year equating to two people, every minute, of every day. It is said that at least six members of family and friends suffer serious emotional effects by this tragic end which means that, year in and year out, six million people must keep their torment silent.

Al Alvarez, who has stood on the brink himself also experienced the trauma of losing his friend and noted poet, Sylvia Plath, to suicide. He describes: 'Suicide is still suspect but in the last eighty odd years a change of tone has taken place: odium, like patriotism, is no longer enough. The suicide prejudice continues but the religious principles by which it once was dignified now seem less altogether self-evident. As a result, the note of righteous denunciation has been modified. What was once a mortal sin has now become a private vice, another 'dirty little secret', something shameful to be avoided and tidied away, unmentionable and faintly salacious, less slaughter than self-abuse.'

A mother who lost her child to suicide was quoted in *The St. Louis Post-Dispatch* as saying angrily: 'You can talk about it if a student dies in a car accident. You can talk about it if a student dies of cancer. You can honour them. You can plant a tree in memory of them...but with suicide (the attitude is) you can't talk about it.' (endnote: Kitch Carolyn and Hume Janice (2008) *Journalism in a Culture of Grief* Routledge UK Quoting from Hesman T. (2005 December 14) Treating an illness, fighting a stigma. St Louis Post-Dispatch p.A1)

Research into suicide is gathered around coroners' verdicts, geographical catchment areas, male and female, conclusive methods and mental health issues. The integrity of statistics has been questioned by academics for centuries. All this to try and halt an act that man has indulged in since time began. It is seen as a signal of what is wrong with society. As Alvarez writes:

'The higher the suicide rate, the greater the social tension and unease. Suicide, that is, interests them only inasmuch as it teaches them about the nature of society. By implication, it is a problem that can be solved by social engineering, social conscience, social concern and genuinely enlightened social services.' Alvarez goes on: 'It seems to me that even the most elegant and convincing sociological theories are somehow short-circuited by this simple observation that suicide is a human characteristic, like sex, which not even the most perfect society will erase.'

In literature the subject is explored and largely romanticised: a predictable demise for the pain of lost love or the gallantry of freedom fighters to become martyrs. Never has it been portrayed simply as it is: a tormented choice to free yourself from the life you are in; an intolerable injustice misunderstood by

February

Sussex Fri 29/02/08 F Body located ? ?
09.10

March

MR Tue 04/03/08 F Body recovered ? ?
EBH Fri 14/03/08 M Body identified 27 Scotland
Pub:15/03/08 14.45

April

MR Fri 11/04/08 F Body recovered
Argus Mon 21/04/08 F Body found ? ?
Pub:22/04/08 20.00

May

EBH Thur 01/05/08 M Michael Patrick Taylor 51 Peacehaven
Pub:19/05/08 and 11/12/08 08.00
EBH Sun 04/05/08 F Body found 30s
Pub:06/05/08 07.00
Argus Tues 06/05/08 M Terry Windsor 65 Peacehaven
Pub:14/05/08 17.45
Argus Sat 10/05/08 F Julie White 46 Shrewsbury
Pub:14/05/08 15.10
ERNLI Tues 13/05/08 M David Richard Frost 44 Essex
Pub:22/05/08 09.37
EBH Thurs 15/05/08 M Wayne Andrew Ashton 41 Hailsham
Pub:22/05/08
EBH Sat 17/05/08 M Syreous Ramezan 44 Tottenham
Pub:19/05/08 18.00
MR Sat 24/05/08 ? Body recovered

June

EBH Thur 19/06/08 M Renaud Champion 51
Pub:01/11/08 Tied his legs together then was witnessed diving off the edge
Argus Sun 22/06/08 M Mark Gordon Roberts 43 Surrey
Pub:22/06/08 19.30
Argus Mon 30/06/08 F Body found ? ?
Pub:30/06/08

July

EBH Sat 26/07/08 M Giles Parker 37 ?
Pub:12/08/08 10.40
One unreported BHCT

August

EBH Mon 25/08/08 M Body recovered ? ?
Pub:26/08/08

EBH Mon 25/08/08 M Geoffrey Monk 77 Oxfordshire
Pub:26/08/08 Drove his car over as the other body was being recovered

September

EBH Sat 06/09/08 M Russell Baker 37 ?
Pub:11/09/08 Tried to drive his car off but ended up jumping

ERNLI Sun 21/09/08 F Julie Simmons 52 Langley
14.31

One more reported BHCT

October

ERNLI Sun 05/10/08 Body recovered ? ?
11.52

November

EBH Sun 16/11/08 Susan Meldrum 46 ?
Pub:25/11/08 10.00

One more reported by BHCT

December

EBH Wed 03/12/08 Mark Richard Baxendine 40 Eastbourne
Pub:24/12/08 12.00

One more reported by BHCT

Two more were recovered further down the coast at Saltdean and two were rescued.

2009

January

ERNLI Sat 24/01/09 M Body located ? ?
15.28

February

EBH Tues 24/02/09 M Guy Ramsey 18 Dorset
Pub:06/03/09

March

Sussex Wed 11/03/09 F Body found ? ?

EBH Sun 22/03/09 F Body found ? ?
Pub:28/03/09

April

Argus Sun 05/04/09 M Body found ? ?
Pub:06/04/09

ERNLI Tues 21/04/09 M Benoit Zanchetti 25 Sussex
Pub:29/10/09 Stabbed himself in the chest then walked to the cliffs

May

ERNLI Thurs 14/05/09 M Jonathan Bramsdon 40 London
Pub:17/09/09

Argus Sat 23/05/09 M Nigel Hammersley ? Dorset
Pub:25/05/09

NHRNLI Thurs 28/05/09 M Body found ? ?

Argus Sun 31/05/09 M&F Neil &Kazumi Pattick 34/44 Wilts
Pub:01/06/09 Son Sam found in a rucksack

June

EBH Sun 21/06/09 M Body found ? ?
Pub:24/06/09

EBH Thurs 25/06/09 M Mark Rumaner 49 Brighton
Pub:16/01/10

July

EBH Sun 05/07/09 F Nora-Ann Westwood 31 Polegate
Pub:05/08/09

EBH Wed 29/07/09 M Gregory Crowhurst 56 Herts
Pub:31/07/09

August

EBH Mon 03/08/09 F Janet Rosemund 59 Bournemouth
Pub:29/01/10

September

Argus Thurs 10/09/09 F Jane Hansen 58 New York
Pub:17/09/09

Argus Fri 18/09/09 M James Handley 23 Folkestone
Pub:24/09/09

Argus Mon 21/09/09 M Matthew Elvidge 23 Hampshire
Pub:24/09/09

EBH Wed 30/09/09 M David Hardill 64 Surrey
Pub:29/01/10 Body not found until 04/10/09

October

MR	Sun 18/10/09	M	Body found	?	?

November

MR	Thurs 12/11/09	M	Body found	?	?
EBH	Sat 14/11/09	M	Shot himself and his dog	50	Shoreham

Pub:31/12/09

December

EBH	Tues 29/12/09	M	Body found	?	?

Wish them peace.

MR	Maritime Rescue Coordination Centre
EBH	Eastbourne Herald local paper
Argus	The Argus local paper
ERNLI	Eastbourne RNLI
NHRNLI	Newhaven RNLI
Sussex	Sussex helicopter

LAMENTS

Louis de Bernieres, after a visit to Beachy Head was moved to write:

> *'I had to leave Beachy Head. Every human being has known times of the most abject and implacable despair, and it was impossible not to feel profoundly what was in the hearts of those sorrowing souls. Knowing and imagining, I found it hard to keep back the tears even though the place is lovely. Either their infinite pain is imprinted upon the atmosphere or one has the illusion that it is. All about are the wisps and traces of broken hearts, cancelled dreams, abandoned expectations. Here are the ghosts of those who loved others too much or themselves too little, of those lost battles with insanity, of those driven to heartsickness by an oppressive sense of futility and the apparent absence of God, of those who defiantly and courageously denied a terminal illness its tortures. Here also are the sad small ghosts of those whose existence nobody noticed until they became a mess to clear away.'*

(Harpers 1996)

Friedrich Engels and Karl Marx are evidenced as sitting on Beachy Head discussing the communist manifesto many times. When Engels was cremated his dying wish was to have his ashes scattered over the cliffs.

Charlotte Smith (British women romantic poets' project) had her work 'Beachy Head: with Other Poems' published posthumously in 1807.

Excerpt:

At day-break, anxious for the lonely man,
His cave the mountain shepherds visited,
Tho'sand and banks of weeds had choak'd their way-
He was not in it; but his drowned cor'se
By the waves wafted, near his former home
Receiv'd the rites of burial. Those who read
Chesl'd within the rock, these mournful lines,
Memorials of his sufferings, did not grieve,
That dying in the cause of charity
His spirit, from its earthly bondage freed,
Had to some better region fled forever.

A more modern poet John Sokol published his vision on 17/12/03 www.pretendingtoswim.com/justlikeheaven.htm

Here at Beachy Head, just south of the White cliffs
of Dover, this chalky bluff
drops five hundred feet to the jagged rocks below.
Ever since the fifth century, thousands have jumped from this peak that sits
in alignment
with coordinates of nearby Stonehenge. From the
sea and the rocks,
the ghosts of dead Druids seem to call to the living
like Circle to Odysseus.
some people drive over the edge in their cars,
others run headlong and leap
like track stars in the Long Jump; many stand at the
precipice and dive
Hail Mary. There are the swan-divers and the
cannon-ballers,
the reverse-two-and-a-halfers, the sliders and
cliff-bouncers
who change their minds too late. There are the
timorous,
who go gently, who inch their way backwards, then
hold on for hours
until they are rescued or until they drop. There are
the curiosity-seekers,
who go only to peer over the edge, but never return.
Screamers and stoics,
teenagers, housewives and tourists, doctors and
farmers: each year -
drowning in life - they jump into the deep

end.

AND
Ssh.anon 06/07

I stand on the brink
At the cliff
Of death and despair.
Mad at the world
Mad at myself
Just mad they say
Lock me away
With them
The others
Locked away.

I can I will I do
Like marriage vows
Promises;
With future deceives
To lie,
To lie in wake
On the brink
Until I chose
Finally.

Willow peace
So sought
Less found
The road to nowhere patterned in

I hear the sirens
And remember
The other world I inhabit
Roaming with the tortured and desperate
Entering their lives
Trying to
Enchant them.
I failed.

Lead me not
Not into temptation, but
Deliver me from evil
For thine is my choice
My power and my glory
For now and
Finally
Forever.
No Amen.

Rejoice:
Today
The sun in my eyes
Doesn't blind me
The wind in my hair
Doesn't send me
Not Today anyway.

Bibliography

Alvarez A. (2002) *The Savage God. A study of suicide.* London: Norton Paperback (First published 1971)

Bathurst B. (2005) *The Wreckers. A story of killing seas, false lights and plundered ships.* London: Harper Collins

Durkheim E. (1966) *Suicide. A study in Sociology.* London: Routledge & Kegan Paul Ltd (First published 1952)

Fortune D. (2001) *Psychic Self-Defence.* Boston: Red Wheel/Weriser (First published 1930)

Giovacchini P. (1981) *The Urge to Die.* New York: Macmillan Publishing Co., Inc

Hawton K & van Heeringen K, eds (2002) *The International Handbook of Suicide and Attempted Suicide.* West Sussex: John Wiley & Sons Ltd (First published 2000)

Joiner T. (2005) *Why people die by suicide.* USA: Harvard University Press

King Francis. (1970) *Ritual Magic in England (1887 to the present day).* London: Neville Spearman Ltd

Kitch C. and Hume J. (2008) *Journalism in a Culture of Grief.* Oxon: Routledge (First published 1987)

Shneidman E. S. (1996) *The Suicidal Mind.* New York: Oxford University Press

Shneidman E. (1994) *Definition of Suicide.* London: Jason Aronson Inc.

Surtees J. (1997) *Beachy Head.* East Sussex: SB Publications

Williams M. (2001) *Suicide and Attempted Suicide.* London: Penguin

Valiente D. (1987) *Witchcraft for Tomorrow.* London: Robert Hale Ltd (First published 1978)

Further reading

Alexander V. (1998) *In the wake of Suicide. Stories of the people left behind.* San Francisco: Jossey-Bass Publishers.

Hesleton P. (2004) *Leylines - A Beginners guide.* London: Hodder & Stoughton (First published 1999)

Hole G. (1945) *Witchcraft in England.* Great Britain: Cedric Chivers Ltd

Newman P. (1997) *Lost Gods of Albion. The Chalk Hill-figures of Britain.* Great Britain: Robert Hale Ltd

Oldridge D. (2000) *The Devil in Early Modern England.* Great Britain: Sutton Publishing Ltd

Picton B. (1971) *Murder, Suicide or Accident.* London: Robert Hale & Company

Rinpoche S. (1992) *The Tibetan Book of Living and Dying.* USA: Harper San Francisco

Simpson L. (2005) *The Healing Energies of Earth.* London: Gaia Books (First published 2000)

Young J. K. (2005) *Sacred Sites of the Knights Templar.* USA: Fair Winds Press (First published 2003)

Wertheimer A. (2000) *A Special Scar. The experience of people bereaved by suicide.* London:Routledge (First published 1991)

References

Allchorn Pleasure Boats
For a unique, close-up view of the famous lighthouse and the magnificent cliffs head to Eastbourne beach. Since 1861 Allchorn pleasure boats have enchanted visitors with a 45-minute daytime round trip from May to October.
http://www.allchornpleasureboats.co.uk

Association of Lighthouse Keepers
You don't need to be lighthouse keeper to get involved.
The association runs a forum for anyone interested in lighthouses, lightships and maritime aids. They host International Lighthouse Day every August and offer regular visits to lighthouses around the British coastline. They also kindly provided the photographs of the Beachy Head Lighthouse Keepers from their vast archives.
http://www.alk.org.uk

Beachy Head Countryside Centre

Next to the Beachy Head Freehouse pub is a charming shop wholly run by volunteers.

Pop inside to experience the history of the Downs and Beachy Head, or pick up gifts, maps and walking guides. Wander through to the Sussex Gallery which features unique arts and crafts by local artists and a permanent exhibition by members of the Chasely Trust, a charity for people with severe physical disabilities.

There is a pay and display car park.

Opening hours:

Jan - March: Saturday, Sunday and school holidays 11am - 3pm

April 4th - October: Every day 10am - 4pm

Nov - Dec: Tuesday, Wednesday, Saturday, Sunday 11am - 3pm

December 26th - Jan 3rd: Every day 11am - 3pm

Telephone: 01323 737273

www.beachyhead.org

Beachy Head Chaplaincy Team (BHCT)

The Shiloh Centre, 80 Wish Hill, Willingdon, Eastbourne, East Sussex BN20 9HA. Pastor Ross Hardy was blessed with a 'vision' to help save lives on Beachy Head. From this he formed the BHCT who began their suicide watch on August 4th 2004 with 6 volunteers patrolling the headland from 18.45 to midnight. In spring 2007 two more full-time pastors were employed and the number of volunteers had increased to 12. The team now has 19 volunteers and 3 full-time pastors who patrol 100 hours a week backed up by a dedicated 24 hour on-call team.

www.bhct.org.uk

Befrienders worldwide with Samaritans

In 2003 the Samaritans (UK & ROI) took on the Befrienders Worldwide network of 401 volunteer centres in 38 countries. Offering the same emotional support to all those in need with confidential help in a non-judgmental environment. This global-linking project also aims to gather and share information and help raise awareness of issues around emotional health and suicidal behaviour.

http://www.befrienders.org/archives

Belle Tout Information Resource

Is a website designed and run by Rob Wassell with in-depth information and stunning photos of the old lighthouse. Many of Rob's photos are featured in this book, with very grateful thanks.

http://www.belletout.org.uk

Belle Tout Lighthouse Hotel
A magnificent, recently refurbished bed and breakfast high on the cliffs of Beachy Head with panoramic views across the Channel.
Telephone 01323 423185
http://www.belletout.co.uk

British Women Romantic Poets Project
Beachy Head: with Other Poems: London
Charlotte Turner-Smith (1749-1806)
www.digital.lib.ucdavis.edu/projects/bwrp/Works/SmitCBeach.htm

Coroner Reform: The Government's Draft Bill
http://www.dca.gov.uk/legist/coroners_draft.pdf

Coroners and Justice Act 2009
Ministry of justice
http://justice.gov.uk

The Coroners' Society of England and Wales
www.coroner.org.uk

Department for Constitutional Affairs
Statistics on deaths reported to coroners, England and Wales, 2006
Richard Allen
http://www.dca.gov.uk/statistics/coroners.htm

Eastbourne Local Historical Society
Grateful thanks especially to Jay Dixon for her invaluable help.
Also John Markwick and George Fairbrother
http://www.eastbournehistory.org.uk

East Sussex Suicide Prevention Strategy 2004-2009. Draft 3
8/10/04 Dr Jennifer Bennett
Claudine Chaloner. Head of Audit and Effectiveness Health and Social Care. Governance Support Team. Sussex Partnership NHS Trust
Claudine.chaloner@sussexpartnership.nhs.uk

Eric Steel
Producer/Director
Easy There Tiger
Working with The Independent Film Channel, Eric Steel made his directorial and documentary debut with a controversial film called *The Bridge*. For one

year he filmed events at the Golden Gate Bridge, San Francisco, a notorious suicide hotspot. The harrowing scenes of attempted and completed suicides were recorded forever. Interviews with relatives and friends were also included. Far from being ghoulish, it is sensitively filmed and narrated and will provoke discussion and analysis which may help with future preventative measures for this unfortunate place.
www.thebridge-themovie.com

John Surtees
Occasional Review. *Suicide and accidental death at Beachy Head.* Br Med J 1982: 284:321-324
His paper from 1982 is still the most quoted reference for research at Beachy Head

Jumpers at Beachy Head
John Sokol
December 17th 2003
www.pretendingtoswim.com/justlikeheaven.htm

Keith Lane
Keith's wife Maggie tragically died at the cliffs in 2004. Overcoming grief and dark depression he has been a lone presence at Beachy Head patrolling at dawn and dusk for people in despair. So far he has saved 29 people from jumping from the cliffs and has received many awards including the Royal Humane Society Award. Keith is now happily re-married to the lovely Val and has a new grandson.

Library enquiries
East Sussex County Council

Louis de Bernieres
Harper's Magazine
Legends of the fall; Beachy Head, England, a popular suicide spot.
January 1996

Mark Hunter
Lighthouse keeper who served at Beachy Head in 1974. Over 30 years later he remembers vividly his time manning the light.

Mary Sisters
Evangelical Sisterhood of Mary
http://www.kanaan.org

Mind
For better mental health
Extract from issue 140 (Jul/Aug 2006) A happy time?
Emma Hickabottom

National Suicide Prevention Strategy for England 2002
http://www.dh.gov.uk/archives
Publication: Suicide audit in PCT localities.

Local suicide audits.
www.csip-plus.org/RowanDocs/SuicideAuditTool.

Guidance on action to be taken at Suicide hotspots.
http://www.csip-plus.org.uk/RowanDocs/SuicideHotspots.pdf
http://www.nimhe.csip.org.uk/

Office for National Statistics
22/2/07 - Corrected - Suicide rates in the UK 1991-2004
http://www.statistics.gov.uk/archives

Trends in suicide by method in England and Wales 1975-2001
http://www.statistics.gov.uk/archives
info@statistics.gov.uk

Emma Gordon
Health geography
Healthgeog@ons.gov.uk

Paul Zwierzanski
For his kind permission to use stories from his website
http://yeoldesussexpages.com

Richard Platt
For his kind permission to use stories from his website
http://www.smuggling.co.uk

Charlie Davies-Gilbert
A lovely, informative website all about Beachy Head
http://beachyhead.org.uk

Roehampton University London
I was lucky enough to study for a MA in creative and professional writing at this stunning university as a mature student. It was while studying here I was inspired to research and write this book under the watchful and patient eye of Susan Greenberg. Have a look at their website for your own inspiration into the creative world of writing.
http://www.roehampton.ac.uk

Rob Wassell
Rob kindly allowed me to use his stunning photographs from his flickr account and through his company RAW - Systems Ltd has created my website. Many, many thanks to him for his support and guidance. If you want to have created a tailor-made, professional and eye-catching website, go to
http://raw-systems.com

Royal National Lifeboat Institution (RNLI)
Eastbourne is the third busiest lifeboat station in the country. It has an All Weather Lifeboat, The Royal Thames, moored in Sovereign Harbour Marina and an Inshore Lifeboat, housed on Royal Parade run by Lifeboat Operations Manager Paul Metcalfe.
Mark Sawyer is a full time Coxswain and Lifeboat Training Coordinator. In 2002 he was awarded the RNLI's Silver Medal for saving the lives of the crew of a sailing yacht, Paperchase, when it foundered in October gales.
http://www.eastbournernli.org.uk/archives
http://www.newhavenlifeboat.co.uk/

Rye Museum
http://ryemuseum.co.uk

Stuart McNab
Special thanks to a brave and discreet man who continues to descend the cliffs in search of the most tragic people and return them to their families for dignified burial. Alongside is his dedicated team of the Eastbourne cliff rescue.

Tad Friend
Staff writer
New Yorker
Letter from California
In October 2003, Tad Friend wrote an in-depth article called *Jumpers.* The fatal grandeur of the Golden Gate Bridge. This was the inspiration for Eric Steele to film *The Bridge.*
www.newyorker.com/archive/2003/10/13/031013fa_fact?/archives

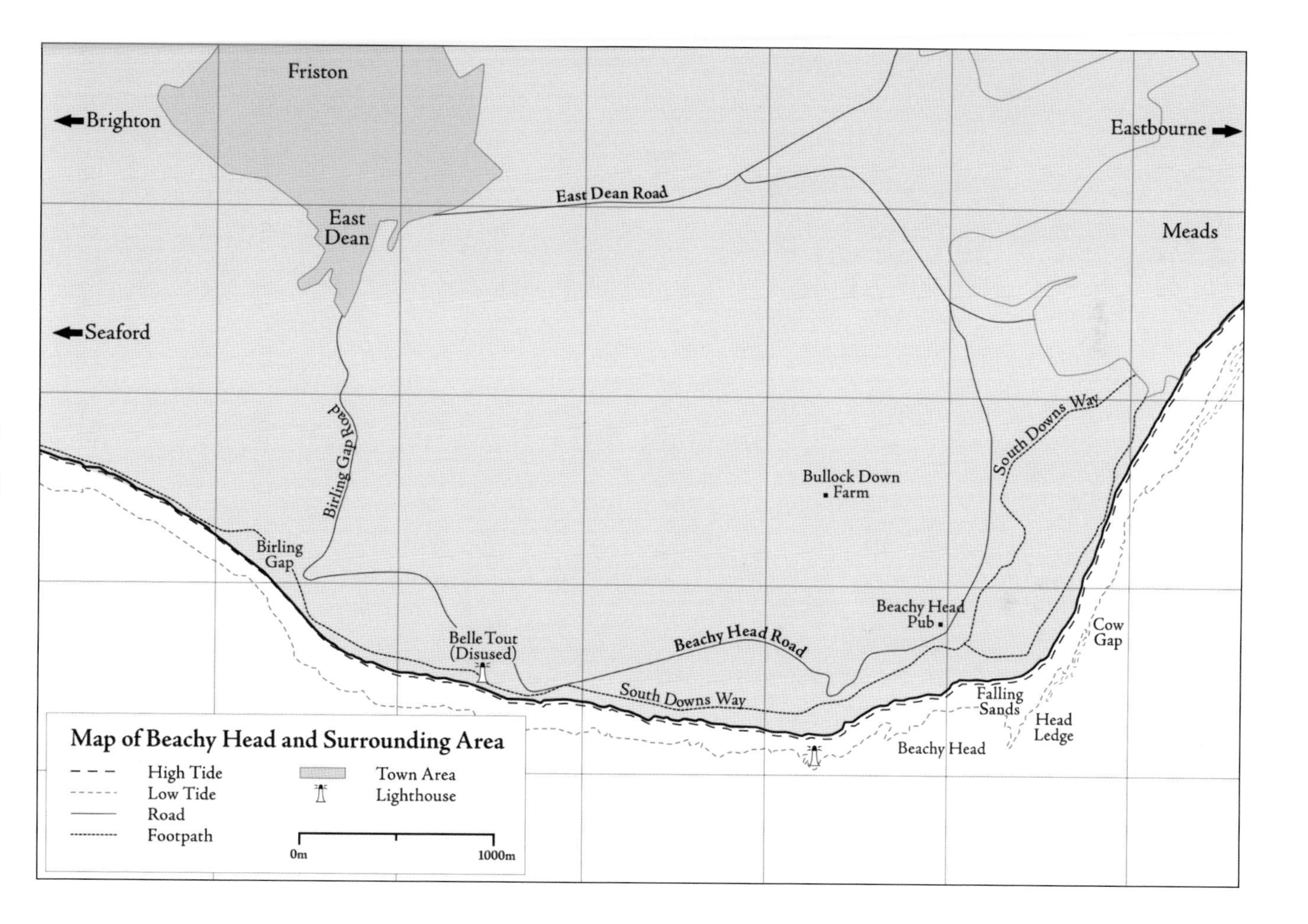

Map of Beachy Head and Surrounding Area
High Tide
Low Tide
Road
Footpath
Town Area
Lighthouse
0m
1000m
Brighton
Seaford
Eastbourne
Meads
Friston
East Dean
East Dean Road
Birling Gap Road
Birling Gap
Belle Tout
(Disused)
Bullock Down
Farm
Beachy Head
Pub
Beachy Head Road
South Downs Way
South Downs Way
Cow
Gap
Head
Ledge
Falling
Sands
Beachy Head

Standing at the edge. © K. J. Varney